D0603785

WEDDING CEREMONIES

ETHNIC SYMBOLS, COSTUME AND RITUALS

Translated from the French by David Radzinowicz Howell
Copy-editing and typesetting: Corinne Orde

Originally published as *Noces* © 2001 Flammarion
English-language edition © 2001 Flammarion

ISBN 2-08010-699-6
FA0699-01-VIII
Dépôt légal: 11/2001

All rights reserved. No part of this publication may be reproduced in any form or by any means, electronic,
photocopy, information retrieval system, or otherwise without written permission from the publisher.

Printed in Italy

WEDDING CEREMONIES

ETHNIC SYMBOLS, COSTUME AND RITUALS

TIZIANA AND GIANNI BALDIZZONE

Flammarion

CONTENTS

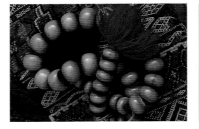
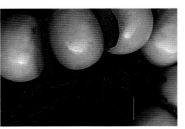

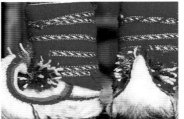

p. 103

p. 119

p. 137

p. 165

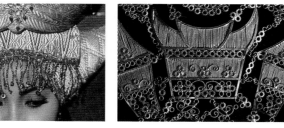

p. 187

What vows do Tibetan brides make as they plait turquoises into their hair? Why do brides in Fez, Morocco, cover their head and body in pearls? What is the origin of the silver jewelry worn by the Black Miaos of China? Who are the *neggafa*s of Morocco? And why do the Tuaregs allot the task of applying the bride's make-up to the blacksmith's wife?

The replies to such questions are often to be found in the myths, legends, and superstitions of a bygone age. Beyond the religious and social aspects of the ceremony, weddings rites and traditions often have the goal of ensuring good fortune for the happy couple and of protecting them from harm.

The tradition of wearing "something old, something new, something borrowed, something blue," for instance, derives from an old Italian saying originally designed to bring the bride good luck and make the birth of a male heir more likely. Among the Black Miaos of Guizhou, it is believed that silver keeps malevolent demons at bay. In Morocco, meanwhile, henna—known as the "powder of paradise"—not only beautifies a spouse's hands and feet but also acts as a defense against the evil eye.

Wedding ceremonies differ widely from country to country, as do the rituals of the wedding procession, the rules behind courtship, and the marriage arrangements, as well as the form taken by the vows themselves. Equally wide is the choice of materials from which nuptial accessories are made, each with its own special meaning: the gold in which the spouses of the Minangkabaus are swathed harks back to the pomp and ceremony of royal weddings of the past, when Sumatra was known as the "Isle of Gold," whereas jasmine, with its heady, sensual perfume, is an integral part of matrimonial hairstyling among the Tamils. Among the nomads of Tibet, girls awaiting marriage wear their hair in thick plaits, while those about to wed sport a special coiffure: one hundred and eight tiny tresses adorned with a band of coral and turquoise. With nails painted in red henna, a young Minangkabau woman shows she is soon to be married. A Peulh Bororo paints his face in ochre in order to attract the fair sex, while a Small Flowery Miao man seeks to prove both his courage and his skill by the pheasant plumes that he wears on his head.

The following pages offer a chance to discover some of these nuptial rites and traditions. Fortunately, many cultures have wisely preserved their own practices right up to the present day, in spite of the effects of globalization.

Of course, the present publication can hope only to lift a corner of the veil that hides the happy couple and their wedding ceremony. It was no easy task to gain the confidence of the betrothed and their families. We have always tried to be discreet, but we are aware that a book such as this does indeed constitute an intrusion into one of the most significant moments of any person's life. All we can hope is that our accounts have been faithful to the desires of all those who were kind enough to open their homes and put their trust in us.

Tiziana and Gianni Baldizzone

As its sensual fragrance has always been associated with marriage, jasmine forms an integral part of the nuptial headdress of a Tamil bride.

The *rakoli*, the jewel to which the bride's flowery headdress is attached.

JASMINE
The Tamils of South India

A fastener representing Surya, the Sun.

Jasmine flower harvest.

We met Sarangan and Jyoti the day before their wedding. Both belong to the orthodox Brahman Shivaite of Tamil Nadu. They had only recently met each other for the first time, but, contrary to what one might have thought, they seemed neither sad nor even resigned: in fact, their families were obviously delighted and both fiancés were beaming with joy.

More an alliance between two families than a true love match, traditional marriage in India is often still arranged. It is the parents who choose a spouse for their son or daughter, basing their decision on a comparison of the couple's horoscope, their respective family trees, fundamental values like respect, education, the nature and inclinations of the two young people, and last but not least, the temperament of the fiancé's mother. Though less the case than formerly, a wife still lives very much under the thumb of her mother-in-law. More often than it is thought in the West, however, the young people themselves are involved in the arrangements for such marriages, and the union is often a happy one. Sarangan, a computing engineer, and Jyoti, a graphic designer, are about to to start a new life together in the United States, but both find it quite natural to accept the betrothed chosen by their respective families. Sarangan's mother, a devout woman particularly well versed in astrology, supervised the comparison of the two horoscopes and made sure that they were compatible.

Once any astral obstacles had been excluded, the two families contacted each other to check the chances of success of a match to which the stars, at least, expressed no objection; it was then up to the priests and astrologers to calculate the most propitious date for the wedding day.

The *thalai*, with the pendant known as *chutti*, that Tamil brides wear on their forehead.

The first invitation is sent to Ganesh, the benevolent elephant-headed deity who, it is said, "removes all obstacles." On the day fixed for the beginning of the wedding ceremonies, we made our way to Sarangan's house. Dawn had not yet broken. On the threshold, floral patterns or *kolam*, which the women had drawn with rice flour and brick powder, hailed the gods, inviting them to descend to earth for a day to bless the happy couple. Sarangan, feeling a trifle awkward in his scanty cotton *dhoti*, was waiting for the arrival of the family priest, who was to celebrate the engagement rites. Smoothing the path for the nuptial ceremony, the *Vagdanam* occurs a day before the wedding proper. The contract between the two families is finalized and sealed, the parents solemnly declaring that the union between their two children will indeed take place.

Beforehand, in the privacy of their respective houses, the fiancés had addressed a prayer to Ganesh, symbolized by a cone of tamaris powder placed on a betel leaf, invoking each of his one hundred and eight special names. They then paid homage to their ancestors and tutelary gods, offering the gifts normally associated with such honorable guests: water, flowers, betel, and *kum kum*. Finally, as a sign that each is henceforth to renounce his or her ego, they break a coconut (the fruit of purity *par excellence*) in two. An integral part of Hindu nuptial rites, the coconut represents the four elements: the shell stands for the earth, the space above the milk for the ether, the milk itself for water, and the sound it makes as it is split, the wind.

Dawn was breaking as the small procession of cars—the modern equivalent of the carts, horses, and elephants of the marriage cortèges described in the *Rigveda*—made its way to the place chosen for the wedding, a vast foyer in a hotel hired specially for the occasion.

A picture of Ganesh made of jasmine. Ganesh is a benevolent god to whom the first invitation to a Tamil wedding is sent.

RIGHT AND FOLLOWING PAGES
The bride prepares for her wedding day.

Jyoti's mother greeted Sarangan by placing the mark of the *tika*—a red spot drawn in *kum kum*, at once a sign of welcome and a wish for happiness—on his forehead. Escorted by her mother and maternal aunt, Jyoti herself entered the hall draped in a violet and gold moiré-silk sari given by her fiancé's parents. Jasmine fell in waves over her neck as she walked forward, a charming smile on her lips, only slightly shy of the tender and contented way her future husband was gazing at her. "Happy is he who marries a young girl whose voice is like the song of the swan, whose skin is the color of the clouds, and whose gentle eyes flash with gold," wrote Satatapa in an ancient text. For his part, Sarangan was visibly delighted with his bride-to-be.

Standing next to their parents, the young couple looked on as the religious ceremonies that marked the most significant stages of their lives were re-enacted before their eyes: baptism (*Namakarana*) and the first meal (*Anna-Prasana*); the first haircut (*Chuda Karana*); and the day when they were presented with a twisted length of cotton as a symbol of their belonging to the high caste of the Brahmans.

Marriage marks the moment when a man assumes his familial and social responsibilities. For this reason it is for Hindus the most important of all *samskara*, a term that is perhaps best rendered as "sacrament." Derived from the Sanskrit, the word designates a group of rites designed to purify spirit and body. Orthodox Brahman families are very attached to the symbolic repetition of *samskara*, an act absolutely obligatory before marriage, since without it the union can never attain perfection. Moreover, for Hindus, only a man accompanied by his wife is permitted to celebrate the rites before the sacred fire—the symbol of energy and of the female gender in general. Until they are married, young people are restricted to watching their parents pronounce invocations to the ancestors and make offerings of rice, bananas, and silver to Kuladeva, one the forms of the goddess Parvati who embodies the divinities of hearth and home. More than a religious sacrament, marriage constitutes a rite of passage leading to a new conjugal state. It is marked by particular attention to bodily cleanliness: the ritual bath in water mixed with essential oils and tamaris powder has an antiseptic and purifying effect. Emblematic of the state of matrimony, the deep red stains left by henna on the groom's fingers also refer to sexual union.

Since the most favorable time to begin the ceremony had been fixed at six o'clock in the morning, Jyoti began to dress before sunrise. For the Hindu, the determining moment of any event in life, be it for good or ill, occurs at the beginning: the young bride therefore cannot afford to be a minute late. Richly complementing Jyoti's beauty, the room was decked out in an incredible mass of scented flowers: tuberose buds, little pale orange petals of *kanakambaram*, laurel, and garland upon garland of both the local varieties of jasmine—*malligai*, or common jasmine, and *mullai*, which has tiny pink flowers. Jasmine is associated with marriage because of its sensual, heady fragrance, and it forms a crucial part of the bridal headdress among the Tamils.

A hairdresser specially engaged for the occasion attached to Jyoti's neck a piece of gold jewelry. Round in form, studded with pearls and rubies, this type of ornament is known as a *rakoli*. She then wove unopened buds into Jyoti's hair and slipped the long plait of black hair into a tube of thin cardboard over which master garland-makers from Chennai had threaded a delicate network of jasmine petals, *kanakambaram*, tuberoses, aromatic herbs, and colorful ribbons.

Jyoti and Sarangan after the ritual of *varmala*,
during which garlands of flowers are
exchanged and hung round their necks,
symbolizing the bonds that unite the couple.

The rubies and pearls on Jyoti's *thalai*.

With hennaed hands and feet, Jyoti receives with Sarangan the blessing of her family and friends.

Jyoti's sister then adorned the young bride's central parting with a row of pearls and rubies ending in a pendant that fell exactly in the middle of her forehead. She then put the pearl and ruby diadem, the *thalai*, into position and completed the headdress with a pair of broaches representing Surya and Soma, the sun and the moon, a homage to the first Brahman marriage recounted in the *Rigveda*. These ancient writings remind the Brahman that their marriages are the purest form of union. Though the ceremony is complicated, there is ample scope for humor. For example, in what is a traditional Tamil joke, the fiancé is supposed to feign reluctance to tie the knot. Sarangan observed the custom to the letter and pretended that he had had a sudden change of heart and decided instead to repair to Varanasi to complete his religious education. As a counter to his (fake) misgivings, Jyoti's parents listed the many virtues of their daughter and begged him to stay. Exchanging garlands of flowers, Jyoti and Sarangan then enacted the union of body, spirit, and soul. This rite, called *varmala*, represents the physical, moral and social links joining the couple. Then, seated on a swing chair swathed in jasmine flowers, the young newly-weds received the blessing of their parents and their friends.

Jyoti's mother traced clockwise circular signs in the air with a flame—the *aarti*, the ancestral ritual by which Agni, fire, is prevailed upon to witness a ceremony about to begin. Sarangan's mother then makes the same gesture carrying a tray of ochre and saffron-yellow rice balls, placing a few at the feet of the couple to ward off pernicious influences.

Under a canopy set up in the middle of the hall, the Brahmans had lit a sacred fire destined to receive the offerings to the gods. From time to time, they poured a little clarified butter, or *ghee*, over it. Seated side by side in the *mandap*—the place where Agni, the most sincere of

This symbolic act reminds Jyoti
that henceforth she will carry
responsibility for the family.

RIGHT
Jyoti's father during a rehearsal
for a ceremony that re-enacts the
Tamil sacraments that precede
the marriage vows.

FOLLOWING PAGES
The ritual of the *Kanyadhaan* at
which Jyoti's father gives her
away to Sarangan.

Hindu divinities, is called to witness the wedding—and, as instructed by the officiating priests,
Sarangan and Jyoti duly repeated the appropriate Sanskrit verses. Hands clasped, they then
threw offerings of puffed rice, seeds, flowers, and *kum kum* powder into the fire.

When Jyoti's father took his daughter on his knees, thus acknowledging her as his worthy
descendant, and placed her right hand in Sarangan's, thereby formally entrusting her to him
and giving her away, a great feeling of warmth spread throughout the whole company. Shouts
rang out and drums beat so as to cover any sobs that might have been heard during the sepa-
ration, bringing bad luck. On a sign from the Brahmans, the couple stood up to complete the
rituals known as *Agni-pradakshina* and *Saptapadi* or the "seven paces" by which, according
to tradition, the marriage is concluded.

Without physically touching, the young couple held on to each other by a loose piece of
clothing and circled around the fire clockwise, seven times. Sarangan then took the ring that
one of Jyoti's aunts had put on her niece's middle toe and led his wife on a walk of seven paces
before the flames, all the while addressing the deities with seven invocations. With the first of
these they asked that they might be granted enough to eat; with the second that they might
enjoy unfaltering spiritual strength; with the third and fourth for the union to be blessed with
good fortune and happiness; with the fifth that they might be rewarded with children.
The sixth invocation was for their cattle, and the seventh for their religious devotions. After
this, Sarangan raised his wife's right foot and placed it on a stone representing the steadfastness of their union.

At the end of the *Saptapadi* ritual, Sarangan places Jyoti's foot on a stone symbolizing the steadfastness of their marriage bonds.

Finally, bending over his beloved, Sarangan applied to her skin the traditional signs that distinguish married women: the *bindior*—the spot in the middle of the forehead, a symbol of fertility—and the vermilion *sindoor* on the parting down the middle of her head. He then hung around her neck the *mangalsutra*—the silk cord hung with a golden pendant, the emblem of marriage itself that Indian women wear until their husband dies.

By now, evening had fallen, and the last guests had left. Sarangan murmured a few words in Jyoti's ear, and led her outside. Their eyes lifted to the sky, he showed her the Pole Star in the constellation of the Little Bear. And so was the very last nuptial rite accomplished.

Offerings of flowers and rice to Agni, Fire,
summoned to witness the wedding.

Ait Atta brides are particularly proud of their large amber necklaces.

Her face covered by the *abroc*, Fatima crosses the threshold and enters the house on her wedding day.

AMBER
The Berbers of Morocco

The Berbers attribute considerable magic and curative properties to amber.

The bride's feet should not touch the ground on her wedding day; her fingers too are bound by a skein of wool to keep them inactive.

Since it had to be kept secret until the very last moment for fear of witchcraft, the precise date of the wedding of Fatima and Brahim, two young Ait Atta Berbers living in a village in the southern Atlas mountains, was told us only late one night. The guests were gathered at Fatima's home, an adobe house with two inner courtyards, onto which the rooms faced. They lay asleep in rows on straw mats on the ground outside. Meanwhile, in the kitchen, the women were already hard at work preparing an enormous chickpea and lamb couscous with sultanas.

The silence was broken before sunrise by the sound of a drum. Another set up in reply, followed by a third and then a fourth, until the walls themselves seemed to reverberate to the beat. Called forth by this signal, the guests congregated in the courtyard reserved for the men, soon to be joined by later arrivals who crammed in together in the darkness. From time to time, a figure would edge through the crowd carrying a tray laden with mint tea.

We simply couldn't move in the crush and stayed flattened against the wall trying to spot the bride and asking everyone we could where Fatima could have got to, whether she was getting dressed, and, if so, when she would be leaving the women's room. The reply from all sides was: "Soon, soon." But time passed and the sun rose and nothing much happened. A skinny little girl, her hair covered in dust, beat a path to a door on the opposite side of the courtyard where we could just make out a group of women, into whose midst she quickly vanished.

The room, reserved for the sole use of the womenfolk, was shrouded in total darkness. The walls kept in the heat they had absorbed during the previous day and the atmosphere was stifling. Seated on the ground, her face covered by a piece of white muslin, Fatima awaited the preparations for her wedding. There would be three days and nights of feasting to mark her transition from a young girl to womanhood, during which she would move away from the authority of her father and submit to that of her new husband.

Converted to Islam at the end of the eighteenth century, the Berbers are nonetheless almost exclusively monogamous. Although marriage is essentially a contract between two families, it is by no means rare for a young girl to marry a man she has already met, and with whom she has already talked, joked or even danced the *ahwash* or *ahidus*.

Fatima and Brahim are first cousins, a relatively frequent occurrence among the Ait Atta for whom consanguineous marriage is an institution. As custom demands in a community that accords supreme importance to virginity, Brahim had courted Fatima out of doors, in a cultivated field swept by the winds. Such an environment made conversation rather difficult and was hardly conducive to secrecy. In this way, however, the fiancés can talk to each other privately without running the risk of being accused of impropriety by prying eyes.

Fatima keeps silent and stock-still as her hands and feet are painted with the henna the Berbers call the "Powder of Paradise." Since her fingers are wrapped in a skein of white wool there is not much she can do, and she is entirely dependent on the *wazira*, the friend and witness to whom the welfare of the spouse is entrusted until the completion of the marriage ceremony.

The room, by contrast, seethes with activity. One woman busies herself with a vase containing an oil for making Fatima's hair shine, an essential element in Berber eroticism. Meanwhile, another woman brings up a flask of rosewater, a third fetches a *serwal*, the famous cotton pantaloons gathered tight at the knee, while yet another carries in the white muslin bridal chemise, then a broach, a silver pin and a ring. There is also a necklace made of cloves for its beneficial properties.

Her female relations and friends vie with one another to lend Fatima a piece of jewelry, since the common Berber belief is that, by the time it is returned, a little of the spouse's good luck, her *baraka*, has rubbed off on it.

Fatima endures the attentions of the married women as they ring her eyes with kohl and redden her lips with *siwak*, a substance made from the skin of the root of the walnut tree. Fatima's face then vanishes beneath the *abroc*, a kind of red silk two-pointed hood that Berber newlyweds wear until the completion of the nuptial rites, in accordance with the ancient tradition of covering the face of Berber women during the marriage ritual, even though in the normal course of life it can be left exposed.

A symbol of marriage, this length of wool yarn is used both to tie a burden to a mule and to assist in childbirth.

FOLLOWING PAGES
Almonds are thrown to bring the bride good luck.

Fatima's wrists are then laden with the heavy, twelve-pronged silver bracelets, known in Berber as *asbig n iquzzain,* that Ait Atta women wear together with other bracelets with sawtooth edges. Among the Berbers, such silver bracelets are associated with matrimony because their ring-like shape symbolizes the female sex, and because the lunar metal is supposed to protect the wearer from bad luck. Westermarck, in a meticulous record of early twentieth-century Moroccan marriage ceremonies, mentions the custom of placing a silver coin presented by the fiancé under the hand-mill used to grind the grain for the wedding meal. The same superstition underlies the coin that is dropped into the fiancée's right slipper just after the henna ceremony.

From a worn-out old leather trunk, Fatima's mother takes a necklace of large amber balls separated by alternate cloth disks. Reciting a brief prayer, she places it over her daughter's shoulders and then, pushing it free of her neck, lets it fall down her back.

Amber (*lluban*) and copal, a partially fossilized resin similar to amber that originates in Senegal, are both appreciated by the Berbers for their magic powers and medicinal properties. Honey-colored and warm to the touch, a symbol of sweetness, an amber necklace is worn with pride by Ait Atta women and constitutes an important family heirloom. It is worn on wedding days and is then carefully put away until the next family marriage.

Fatima leaves the house to the trill of ululation. Since her feet should never touch the ground on her wedding day, her brother lifts her bodily and places her gingerly in an off-road vehicle, an updated version of the mule that would in earlier times have carried her to the house of her betrothed. The women follow the car, banging on goatskin drums called *tellunt*—the same word as used for their flour sieves. The drumming accompanies the chants intended to bring the bride happiness in her new life and the songs of farewell for the fatherly roof she leaves behind.

Having circumambulated the fiancé's house three times to the deafening accompaniment of firecrackers, drum beats, and ululation, the nuptial procession escorts the bride to a specially prepared chair against a wall. From a skein of white, red, and black wool there hang the objects that make up the dowry. The woolen rope, which is also used to tie burdens to the mule as well as to assist in childbirth, is another symbol of marriage. It is given by a father to his daughter the day she leaves the paternal house to enter that of her future spouse.

The whole village is aquiver, waiting for the "night of virginity." This event, like everything else concerned with female sexual matters, is *hshuma*, a term hard to translate, signifying at the same time shame and modesty.

For Berbers, the wedding night is an occasion of the utmost importance. If the young woman has the duty of remaining a maiden, in exchange, the man has to prove his virility, and only the blood of the hymen can offer undeniable proof. The whole act cannot last too long, however, since all the relations standing together just outside the wedding alcove are waiting impatiently to see the bride's *serwal* spattered with blood, a visible sign that "everything is as it should be." A hymen that fails to bleed, or an erection that fails to materialize, can dramatically sour the atmosphere of what would otherwise have been a joyous feast day.

We were told the story of an unfortunate young man who buckled under the pressure and, sick with nerves, failed to consummate proceedings. His parents, convinced that sorcery lay behind their son's failure to perform, summoned a local fakir who possessed a

A Berber bride's face remains veiled throughout the wedding.

FOLLOWING PAGES
Fatima and her *wazira*, witness and assistant to the bride.

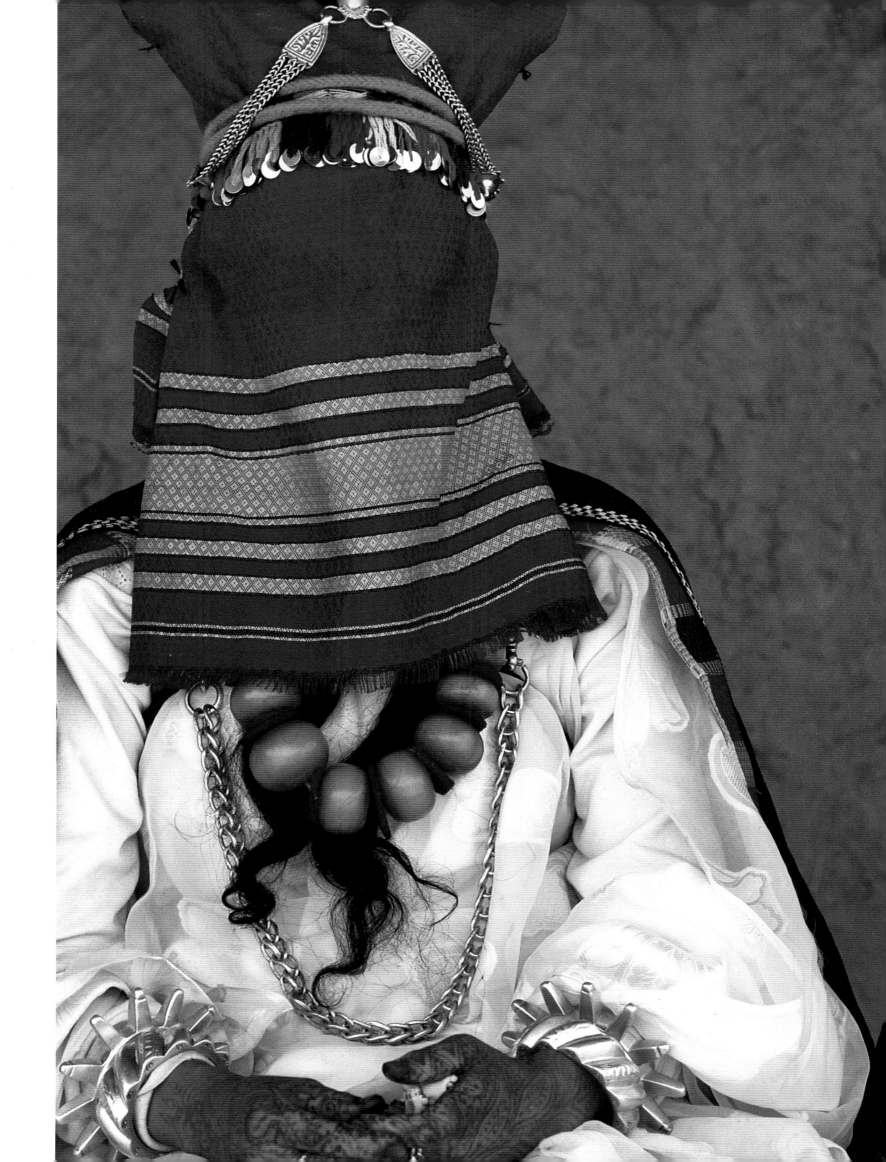

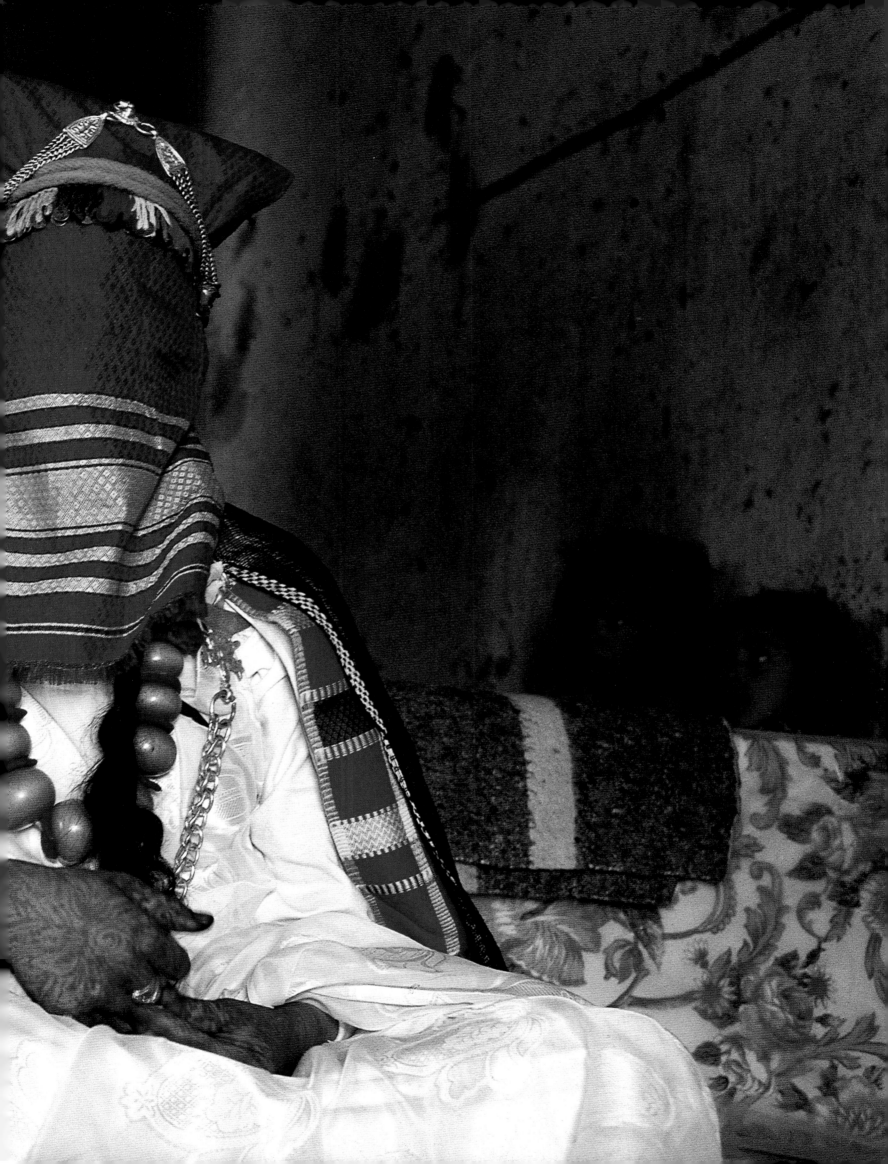

FOLLOWING PAGES
A dance to the beat of the *tellunt*, a drum stretched with goatskin.

surefire remedy. Taking a piece of parchment, on which he had inscribed a few chosen verses of the Qur'an, he dipped it a glass of water so that the ink in which they were written imparted some of the prophylactic power of the holy scripture to the water. Having imbibed the water in which the sacred words had been dissolved, the young man found his virility restored, and both the marriage and the young man's reputation were duly saved from disaster.

The morning after the wedding night, Fatima, still wearing the bloodstained tunic in which she had lost her virginity, spent a number of hours receiving presents and congratulations from the guests. As stipulated by tradition, she would stand up and, holding on to her friend and witness, the *wazira*, would throw a handful of almonds to the children who dive onto the fruits impregnated with some of the bride's good fortune, crying "*baraka, baraka.*"

By the time Brahim appears, resplendent in a white *djellaba*, it has grown late. His arrival signals the beginning of the dance of the *ahidus*. The beating of the *tellunt* redoubles and the women break into full-throated song. The younger boys join ranks, and, elbow to elbow, line up in a long, undulating row in front of the girls who cross their arms across their body, their right hand grabbing that of the girl to their left and vice versa. Their faces

are draped in brightly embroidered black veils and their long tresses bounce up and down on their hips as they stamp to the beat of the drums, their feet sending up clouds of dusty earth. The dance is a sensual affair in which men and women vie with each other in a singing competition, the subjects of which include beauty and love, as well as the odd ironic allusion to village anecdotes.

Fatima and Brahim soon join the group but dance the *ahidus* once only, when they are face to face. Without warning, the chants cease, the rows break up, and the crowd of relations and friends accompanies the couple to the matrimonial house. By the light of a single lantern, Brahim is finally allowed to lift the *abroc* and reveal Fatima's face, drained by the three tense days of incessant heat.

Free of the barrier of Fatima's veil, our eyes can meet at last; our hands touch briefly and we simply smile, feeling no need for words. Then an influx of guests pushes us to one side and Fatima disappears from view once again.

Night, as black as pitch, has already fallen over the southern Atlas.

Fatima dances the *ahidus* flanked by friends wearing embroidered veils.

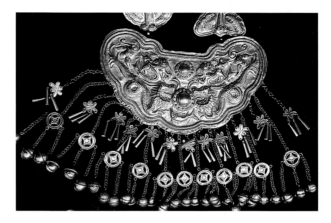

Considered an effective defense against the evil eye, silver is believed to be a good omen for brides.

Wu Mejying on the way to her betrothed's home village.

SILVER
The Black Miaos of China

Silver pendant evoking a legend that recounts how the Black Miaos originally emerged from butterfly eggs.

"There was once a young man
Who caught a golden pheasant in the mountains
As a present for his beloved,
A child who was so poor she had to work
From morn til night every day of the year.
Responding to her suitor's declaration of love,
The young girl dressed up like the beautiful pheasant:
Her hair made into a bun to stand in for his crest;
Full wide sleeves in imitation of his wings;
And, for the tail, she attached colored ribbons around her skirt.
So she appeared to her beloved
As beautiful and as graceful as the golden pheasant."

Wu Mejying too looked as if she'd just walked out of some ancient lyric. It was her wedding day and, accompanied by a few girlfriends, she was making her way along the paths that crisscross the paddy-field terraces in the Leigong hills to the village of Mojian, her fiancé.

As befits a bride-to-be, Wu Mejying's headdress consisted in a garland of flowers ringed by sections of chased metal, from which hung a multitude of silver buds. It was topped by another silver bouquet bristling with butterflies, peacocks, and other birds. She held her arms, quite invisible beneath the billowing sleeves of a loose-fitting coat, close to her sides. As she walked, more than twenty bands embroidered on her skirt waved like the tail of that golden pheasant in the legend, the bird on which the traditional wedding costume of the Miao people is based.

Wu Mejying belongs to the Black Miao community, one of the fifty or so ethnic minorities living on Chinese territory. It was the Japanese ethnologist Tatsezou Taoriyi, author of an early twentieth-century monograph on the customs of the Miaos, who gave them their name, deriving it from the color of the jackets they wear.

The Black Miaos live in small villages scattered over the hillsides of the Leigong that form the backbone of the Miaoling Mountains, a succession of outcrops and gorges that the tropical climate has draped in forests of pine and cedar. It is a land where, as a local saying has it, "no-one has ever seen more than three square feet of flat ground or more than three consecutive sunny days."

Totally cut off from the rest of the country until the not-so-distant past, the isolated Miaos have evolved such a fantastic variety of garments and personal adornments that their costume has become a kind of identity card that can indicate the community to which any given

Before the silver ornament is fixed on Wu Mejying's head, extensions are threaded onto her hair.

individual belongs. Legend recalls that the Miaos lost their indigenous alphabet during one of the migrations that saw them leave the Yellow River basin to settle in southeast Guizhou, where they live today. Without a writing system, the primary means of passing their history down from generation to generation was to create patterns on embroidery. Miao brocades, which already enjoyed great renown more than a thousand years ago under the Tang dynasty, remain even today a valuable form of document for anyone trying to study the legends of a people whose name, romantically enough, means "Sons of the Earth."

Female costume, traditionally embroidered by the wearer herself, is also a weapon of seduction, and is of prime importance in the chase for a husband. Until the relatively recent past, any young girl who did not know how to embroider was condemned to a life of celibacy, since historically, Miao men pay great attention to the costume of any prospective spouse. It is therefore no coincidence that a successful suitor receives as a love token from his intended a piece of the cloth she is embroidering for her wedding dress. For centuries, little Miao girls have been taught the art of embroidery almost from the cradle. By the age of ten or twelve they know all the techniques of flat, plaited, cross, and chain stitch by heart.

Wu Mejying's schooling may have opened other doors to her, but it left her with little or no time to learn the art of needlework like her mother and grandmother before her, so she has been unable to make her own wedding gown. A member of a new generation, her

fingers, fleet enough across the computer keyboard, have not been trained to ply needle and thread, and so her dress was embroidered by the elders of the family. Carefully reinforcing the cloth in the vulnerable areas where the stitching might be prone to wear, the women, with a savoir-faire that dates back millennia, depicted on Wu Mejying's costume much of the mythology, legends, and history of the Miao people. In some parts of the gown, a long strand shows a river that was forded; in others, a zigzag stitch recalls the twisting mountain paths of Leigong; elsewhere, the hem banding the sleeves represents the mighty Yellow River itself from which the population originally springs. The inner sleeve, the edges of the jacket, the ribbons on the skirt, all depict a landscape teeming with colorful figures and allegorical animals, embroidered in running or plaited stitch.

Sacred creatures or animals that bring good luck, such as the mythical phoenix and large centipedes, meet dragons, dragonflies, butterflies, and, of course, fish. The fish is a symbol of plenty and recalls the time when the Miaos, threatened by other, more warlike ethnic groups, envied the life of the river peoples. There also appear the great deeds of the heroine Wu Moxi, who, it is said, cast into the middle of the battlefield seeds that immediately sprouted into warriors armed and ready to fight the Miao cause.

Heralded by the sound of firecrackers and the piping of the *lusheng*, the nuptial procession arrives at the groom's home village at last. Mojian and Wu Mejying cross the last few paddy-fields together in a line behind the three young men sent to fetch the fiancée, as is the custom, and together they clamber up the stone steps between the timber-built houses on the

FOLLOWING PAGES
Wu Mejying, the young bride,
admires her silver headdress.

mountain side. Mojian's parents greet the young bride with a sticky serving of rice and some rice wine. In accordance with tradition, the village women stand a little to one side, commenting audibly on the fiancée's appearance. "She has broad shoulders; she'll be a good worker!" one remarks as she eyes Wu Mejying appreciatively up and down. "She has narrow hips," another observes less charitably, "she'll find childbirth rather tough." "Come, come," interrupted a third, "look at her high cheekbones! They mean good luck and old bones!"

Before being allowed across the threshold, Wu Mejying has to down many a glass of alcohol. Then Mojian's brother tends her an umbrella as a token of good luck and invites her in. Dishes of rice, fish, and pork fat stand on the ancestral shrine. Wu Mejying takes a bite, and then, dousing the pictures of Chiyou with a few drops of rice wine, she offers her homage to the mythical chief who defended the first Miaos against incursions by the forces of Huang Di, the Yellow Emperor. Then, followed by her girlfriends, she enters the room in which a mass of delicacies have been prepared: spare ribs, fish, large boiled lettuce leaves, and, above all, copious amounts of rice alcohol.

For the Miaos, a wedding is an opportunity for a huge feast as much as an occasion to celebrate the rather complicated rites that sanctify their unions. The bride-to-be thus makes her way to the house of her intended, but he remains hidden away, in accordance with the custom

On arriving at her husband's house, Wu accepts the rice balls she is offered to welcome her.

FOLLOWING PAGES
Wu Mejying and Mojian walking across the paddy-fields.

Attire is a weapon of seduction, and silver is
sign of wealth, while embroidery shows the
skill of the woman who made and wears it.

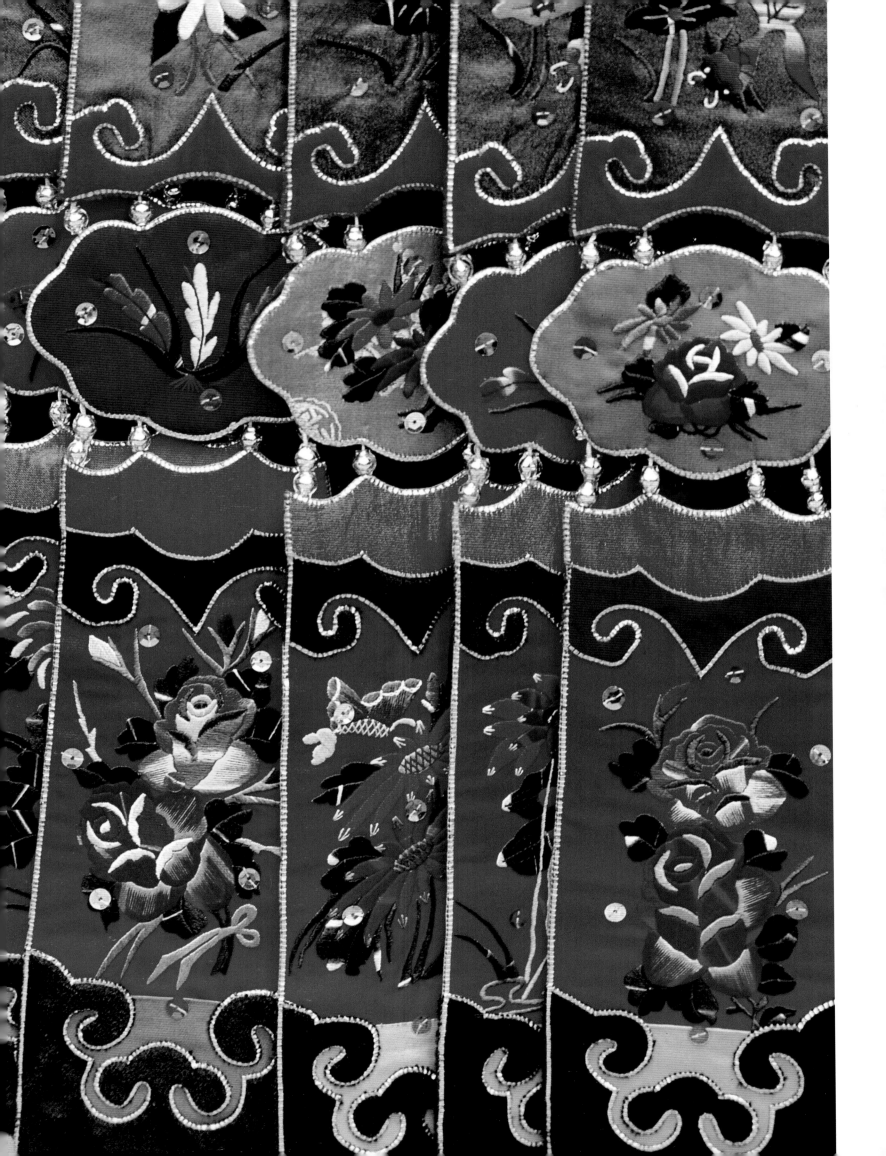

Embroidery and silver ornaments allude to many of the myths, legends, and history of the Miao people.

that forbids him from showing his face in public during the festivities. He is not averse though to throwing a few clandestine glances at his beloved. Miao tradition has it that, after the wedding, the girl returns to the bosom of her own family. The marriage is not consummated until it is time to sow the fields, when she will join her husband in the work. The family will not be truly one, though, until she is expecting her first child; only then does the couple's life together truly begin. Like some Chinese princess, Wu Mejying smiles down regally on the assembled company, seemingly untroubled by the great weight of silver ornaments she is wearing—something like twenty-five pounds of necklaces, bracelets, pendants, broaches, and diadems that cover her from head to foot. These have been made by highly skilled craftsmen. In former times, almost every family could boast at least one such talented artisan.

Considered as effective protection against the evil eye, as well as a strong charm against the tigers that years ago roamed the forests of Guizhou, silver is today worn like a kind of precious good-luck talisman. The origin of the Miaos' taste for silver jewelry in particular is, in fact, something of a mystery. A legend still told in the highlands near Taijiang recounts how, in an age long past, an impoverished young man lived high up in the Leigong hills. He was desperately in love with a girl for whom the parents asked an exorbitant bride-price. How could he ever afford three hundred pigs, three hundred waterbuffalo, and three thousand pounds of rice? The two young people could see no way out and were forced to meet secretly deep in the forest. One night, the girl gave her suitor three thick stalks of sunflower soaked in oil that she asked him to make into torches to light the way home. Once back at his own house, he was stupefied to see that all three stalks had miraculously transformed into three pieces of silver. He ran off to pay homage to his beloved's parents who forged the silver he gave them into sumptuous ornaments that their daughter wore at their wedding feast.

Village elders tell how, since that day, master silversmiths in the Leigong uplands, heirs to a technique going back thousands of years, have been able to work a silver filament until it is as fine as a human hair. On pendants and broaches that will later adorn the bride, the same craftsmen carved some of the animals of the Miao mythological pantheon.

Wu Mejying's dowry also includes one of the bridal ornaments with silver horns that have made Miao women famous. At the center of this extraordinary headdress (worn also by young Miaos at the Chinese New Year), two dragons do battle toe to toe for treasure. A symbol of strength and abundance, the dragon represents Chiyou and is—with the butterfly—a favorite animal figure.

Wu Mejying holds a butterfly-shaped pendant that reminds all present of the ancient legend recounting how the first Miaos hatched from butterfly eggs. She then tells the story of a butterfly who laid twelve splendidly colored eggs. A mythical bird, the *phan*, was so entranced by their beauty that he decided to sit on them until they opened. After some time, the eggs hatched and there emerged a dragon—lord of the waters—a buffalo, a centipede, a snake, a tiger, catastrophes and calamities, happiness and misfortune, and, finally, a Miao man and woman, who were taught how to dance by a dragonfly.

With a cascade of silver flower buds dangling before her laughing eyes, Wu Mejying stands up and removes her heavy adornments as well as her outer wedding garments. She then picks up a pair of buckets, throws a pole over her shoulder, and, in the company of one of her friends, goes down to the brook to take water for her husband's family—her new family.

Flowers and representations of the mythical heroine Wu Moxi on the bridal headdress.

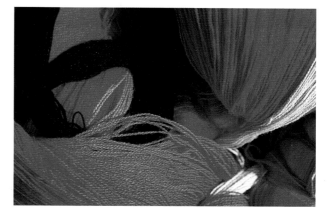

Tiaohuapo, the "dance of the flowery meadows," a festival at which the Miaos strike up relationships with members of the opposite sex.

Girls of marriageable age spend whole days preparing enormous ornamental headdresses made of red wool.

RED WOOL AND PHEASANT FEATHERS

The Small Flowery Miaos of China

Young Miao suitors wear pheasant tail-feathers as proof of their courage and skill.

The Miaos' extravagant wool headcloths.

FOLLOWING PAGES
Preparations at the village for *Tiaohuapo*.

Zhang Fa Xi had always been a gifted huntsman. Everyone in the village envied the collection of pheasant-tail feathers stuck in the headdress that he wore every spring festival. Thanks to such hunting trophies, the girls could all see that he was courageous and adroit. The *Tiaohuapo* was clearly going to present a man like Zhang Fa Xi with ample opportunities of finding himself a woman. The *Tiaohuapo*, or "dance on the flowery meadow," is the love festival that, year in year out, attracts over forty thousand Small Flowery Miao people to the highlands of western Guizhou in the region of Liupanshui. So called because of their traditional floral garb, the Small Flowery Miaos (also known by their French name of "Petites Fleurs") are just one section of the Miao people that the Chinese government has only over the last fifty or so years recognized as a *bona fide* nationality.

The Guizhou Miaos are descendants of mountain people renowned for their courage, pride, and, above all, their fierce independence and adhesion to traditional values. Initially hunter-gatherers, they then practiced a semi-nomadic form of agriculture dependent on slash-and-burn. According to ethnological research, this technique was one reason behind their migration to Southeast Asia, since it obliged them to clear virgin arable land every five years. Following such massive deforestation, the Miaos progressively had to become rice-cultivators and started growing their crops on terraces.

One myth relates that they came originally from Central Asia. During the Yuan Dynasty, under pressure from Mongol incursions, they were gradually forced to emigrate to the provinces of Guizhou and Yunnan. Today they number all together more than four million.

The embroidered shawls of the Small Flowery Miaos bear witness to their exodus, since, if legend is to be believed, the decoration depicts their original homeland. Two brothers, chased from their territory by a particularly vicious war, are supposed to have emigrated south. The elder traveled on horseback while his younger brother, who followed on foot, painted pictures of their lost native land on their garments: the squares symbolized the abandoned fields, the

ABOVE AND PREVIOUS PAGES
Zhang Fa Xi and his trophy of
pheasant plumes.

red lines figured fish, stars, and trees, while two bands, one red and the other yellow, indicated the two longest rivers in China, the Yangtze Kiang and the Hwang Ho (the Yellow River).

Nowadays, apart from in a handful of isolated villages, these traditional shawls, embroidered in colors that would not be out of place in a haute couture fashion house, are worn only on special occasions. Young people are more at ease in T-shirts, jeans, and flashy tops and will even swap a fine embroidered belt for some electronic gadget. This does not mean, however, that they have lost all sense of identity or that they are no longer in touch with tradition. Their customs are reborn practically untouched by the passing of time at festivals such as the "dance on the flowery meadow."

The *Tiaohuapo* offers a veritable feast of matchmaking. Among the Miaos, the art of seduction (which they call *you fan*) comprises music and songs as well as broad smiles and furtive glances. They are renowned experts at it. First the boys send musical messages of love through a bamboo flute or a *lusheng*, a reed-type woodwind instrument that recalls both a flute and an organ. The girls respond with a sequence of modulations played on the harmonicas they always carry with them to express their feelings and to communicate with their loved ones. References to this age-old festival are to be found in texts that date from the seventeenth century and that recount how young people of marriageable age courted, arranged trysts, and built the foundations of their future life together. For Westerners and for the Japanese, the *Tiaohuapo* has become a tourist attraction, while for the Chinese it provides an opportunity

for a picnic and the chance to make an official speech or two. But for the young Small Flowery Miaos themselves, it remains first and foremost a chance to meet others of their age and to put the age-old strategies of seduction into practice.

ABOVE AND FOLLOWING PAGES
Preparing the girls' hair.

Zhang Fa Xi had made his way on foot along the steep paths that connect his village with the hills of Tiaohua. So as not to crease his special white tunic and embroidered shawl, he had folded them both up carefully in a little bundle and slung them over his shoulder. When he had almost reached the hillside he stopped at the edge of a lake to change. All around the lakeside, on the banks of the stream, and on the flanks of the foothills, countless huddles of girls were putting the final touches to one another's outfits. Beyond the reach of prying eyes, one was arranging her friend's hair; another was fastening a short embroidered cape over her shoulder; a third girl was knotting a brightly colored sash around her waist and trying to pull on yet another gathered skirt over all the others she was already wearing. Young Miao girls of northwest Guizhou wear dozens of such batik-type skirts one over the other. Symbols of beauty, they are also intended to show the boys watching on how clever and good with her hands the wearer is.

Batik, or *laran*, means both "wax" and "dyeing" in Chinese, and is a technique of coloring fabric that has been known in China since the time of the Sui and Tang dynasties. It is the Miaos who are supposed to have invented the method over a thousand years ago, and an often-told legend recounts the story of its origin.

Once upon a time, there lived an extraordinarily beautiful but destitute young girl. She was so poor that she possessed neither the finely embroidered dress nor the silver jewelry she needed to join in the festivals, and thus had no hope of finding herself a husband. One day she inadvertently broke a little jar of beeswax that spilt out over a bolt of white cloth she was about to dye with indigo. When she removed the cloth from the dyestuff, she noticed that wherever the wax had fallen the stain had not fixed and pretty white designs appeared on the colored fabric. With a stylus she cut up the rest of the wax and used it to draw patterns of flowers, birds, and clouds with fighting dragons on the cloth. She was then able to run up a spectacularly beautiful dress for herself, and her elegance when she wore it at the spring festival eclipsed that of even the wealthiest girls.

Sporting dyed-wool headcloths of huge size, groups of marriageable young women were steadily arriving from every village on the mountain. This extraordinary headgear, bright red or orange in color, sometimes with yellow, white, or pink stripes, weighs near on twenty pounds. Even with such outsized headdresses framing their girlish faces, Small Flowery Miao maidens stand scarcely more than four foot eight. Married women, who were no longer allowed to wear the special woolen headdress, were appearing in long embroidered capes reaching down to their wrapped feet. Occasionally a small child could be seen hidden within its folds. Within a short space of time, the whole Tiaohua hillside was transformed into a vast garden teeming with flowers.

Zhang Fa Xi, together with the other *lusheng*-players, was waiting for the master of ceremonies, a tiny old man well-versed in the secrets of the ancient tree cults and in all the "flower dances." Headed by the oldest *lusheng*-player, the young men, their hair dressed with long pheasant plumes, made their way to a cement platform erected in the middle of a clearing between two hills teeming with people. On one side stood the Miaos themselves, while on the other, drawn as always by the annual spectacle, the Han Chinese watched the spectacle.

The master of ceremonies came up carrying a branch bedecked in ribbons, lengths of cloth, and paper flowers that the younger men proceeded to plant in the center of the dais. It was only then that the *Tiao Hua*, the dance that gives its name to the whole ceremony, struck up. To the increasingly rhythmic sound of the *lusheng*, the boys began to dance around the flowering branch, making their pheasant-plumed headdresses wave up and down. The energetic movements of this dance appear rather bucolic, since they mimic various rustic tasks as a prayer for a good harvest. For some authorities, the budding tree is throwback to an ancient animist cult that venerated plants as subterranean divinities. For others, it symbolizes a fruit tree beneath which young girls in former times would stand and whisper secrets about their love-life.

Drawn by the singers and *lusheng*-players, the girls in turn surged forward to the sides of the dais, struggling through to the front row to get a chance to attract the young men's attention. By the time the music had stopped, youngsters of both sexes had invaded the dancing area and, revolving clockwise in a swirl of color, were trying to draw as many looks as they could.

Wang Shun Qin, a very young girl scarcely four foot six tall and practically buried beneath her huge crown of red and white wool, skipped passed Zhang Fa Xi and, quick as a flash, snatched at the colored sash of his short jacket. This was a sure sign that he had taken her

Adjusting the red wool headdress.

FOLLOWING PAGES
Girls gathering on the hill for the *Tiaohuapo*.
Dancers carrying *lushengs*, a instrument similar to both the organ and the flute, gathering around the blossoming tree.

fancy. Zhang Fa Xi had been quite a success already and any number of girls were to pull at his sash and invite him to go off with them.

Miao women enjoy a considerable degree of sexual freedom and are allowed to take whomsoever they want as a husband. They can express their feelings freely through rituals of seduction that are nothing if not frank. Lovers swap amorous messages in the form of duets passed down to them from generation to generation, or else ask for their intended's hand with a song they've composed themselves. In the game known as the "hunt the pigtail," the suitor tries to make off with his sweetheart's headdress. If he manages to do so—and if she lets him take it— it means she looks kindly on his suit. A young Miao man can also flirt through any number of love games: "throwing the scarf," an archery contest using an embroidered target (made of course by his belle); or "searching for fruit trees." He can also telegraph his love by blowing across a leaf held between the teeth using a kind of secret language that the Miaos have employed since time immemorial as an invitation to a romantic walk through the woodland.

Groups of young people from neighboring villages strolled about the hills on the hunt for a little dalliance or a sister soul. Zhang Fa Xi had amassed quite a hoard of embroidered scarves, combs, and compact mirrors, each a love token given by a girl fascinated by his skill on the *lusheng*. Arm in arm with a pair of male companions, he paced the hillside inspecting all the pretty girls. Beneath every headdress, however, he was trying to make out the face of the girl who had first yanked at his sash, returning one by one all the tokens he had received from other maidens.

It was a rare cloudless spring day in Guizhou. Seated on a rock, Wang Shun Qin was enjoying the last rays of sunshine that had graced the festival. She followed Zhang Fa Xi with her eyes. Every time it looked as if he was about to come up to her, she would pretend to be absorbed in conversation, but whenever he wandered off again, she would crane her neck trying to catch a glimpse of him. At last the young man made his approach. Wang Shun Qin took out her harmonica and played a short tune. Zhang Fa Xi snatched it from her, piped out a few notes, and ran off, with the girl in hot pursuit.

The men had lit a fire and were smoking their pipes, recounting old legends or more recent stories, while the married women were rocking children to sleep in their arms and the hawkers who sold sugar cane were counting up their earnings for the day. The spectacle proper had come to an end and the tourists had long since left. Tiao Hua hill now belonged to the Small Flowery Miaos alone, to young men and women concealing themselves behind a tree or a rock to get to know each other better or to exchange confidences.

Zhang Fa Xi and Wang Shun Qin had repaired to the lakeside. He had returned her harmonica, while she had surreptitiously slipped a handkerchief into his hand. Then each made their way to their own village. All they now needed to pursue their idyll born in the shade of the blossoming trees of Guizhou was their parents' consent to the wedding.

Two girls waiting for their boyfriends.

FOLLOWING PAGES
A young Miao woman courts her intended by tugging on the sash around his jacket.

Piece of contemporary jewelry which
respects traditional forms.

Fabric ornaments on a Lapp jacket
and bonnet.

RED BONNETS AND REINDEER-SKIN BOOTS

The Lapps

Reindeer-skin boots called *gallokak*.

A wedding following the Lutheran rite, in a church full of guests wearing the red bonnet.

Tacitus called them the *Fenni*, describing them as an "extraordinarily savage and utterly destitute tribe, without weapons, horses, or dwelling places." In the eighth century, the Lombard historian Paul the Deacon wrote that they "lived in a land where in summer the sun shines even at night, but in winter it remains dark all day long."

The Lapps or Sameh—as they prefer to be known—are the earliest surviving inhabitants of the Scandinavian tundra. Some authorities believe them to be of pre-Mongoloid origin, while others believe they traveled up from the Urals, but their roots, their earlier territories, and even their very name are shrouded in mystery. Some maintain that the word Lapp comes from the Swedish *loepa* that means "run, leap"—a reference to the agility with which the Lapps move over the ice and snow on their wooden skis. Others, though, think it more likely that it comes from *lappu*, the "extreme edge."

Inhabiting a boundless territory that straddles Norway, Sweden, Finland, and northern Russia, until the relatively recent past the Sameh lived in rhythm with the migrations and ways of the reindeer, "an animal similar to our red deer," as Paul the Deacon explained. For a people who have to eke out a lonely existence over a vast and unfriendly terrain, dependent on the movements of their flocks, meetings of any sort necessarily offer a rare opportunity to arrange marriages. Asking for a woman's hand is an important event, traditionally accompanied by what may seem to us rather strange practices. In some parts of the country, the young suitor had to go to his intended's parents and, without further ado, prepare them a steaming jug of coffee. If the young woman's parents did not drink it, this signified refusal, and the young man had to be on his way. If, on the contrary, they poured out the coffee until it overflowed down the sides of the cup, it was an unmistakable sign that they regarded the suit favorably. Among the highland Lapps, the two families would celebrate their children's union by striking a flame from two fragments of rock, since, like the sparks that fly from the heart of two flints, children are born from the fire of love that enflames the two young people.

According to Johan Turi (writing in the second half of the nineteenth century), Lapp marriage was arranged by way of barter, a system that included the payment of a bride-price. Accompanied by a sort of guarantor—in general a man wielding some influence within the community—a suitor would visit his beloved's parents. If the girl looked upon him indulgently, the custom was that she would go out to meet him, unharness his reindeer, and welcome him into her tent. After respectful preliminaries, there began tough negotiations over the value of the gifts to be offered in exchange for the young maiden's hand. The guarantor who accompanied the prospective groom defended his cause as best he could by extolling the young man's skill and his other qualities, while the young woman's parents would enumerate their daughter's virtues and so keep the price as high as possible. The duel of words continued until the two parties reached an agreement as to the number of reindeer and hides or the amount of money the suitor had to pay to ensure the girl's hand.

Nowadays, such ancient pre-nuptial agreements have all but disappeared. Nonetheless, although the marriage itself is performed following the Lutheran rite, it is usually just the sanctification of a wedding previously celebrated according to old Sameh traditions, sometimes even after the birth of one or two children has further consolidated the union.

The couple and their guests leaving church after the wedding.

For the Lapps, the Eastertide feasts have always been the optimum time for weddings. At this time their timber-built churches, like that at Kautokeino, are decorated in a dazzling array of colors: red cloth bonnets adorned with hand-woven and embroidered textile ornaments; various hues of yellow, blue, and red silk or woolen shawls fastened by gold or silver clasps; the deep blue of the loose jackets with their tightly pleated hems worn over reindeer-hide breeches that allow the Lapps to sit down in the snow without getting wet and catching cold. Even a husband's wealth can be gauged by the thick belt he wears around the waist. It is decorated with silver and gold coin whose number precisely indicates to a Sameh the rank of the couple and how many head of cattle they possess.

Based on a centuries-old model, Sameh wedding apparel serves today as an outward sign of the people's renewed pride in their ancient traditions. Formerly made entirely of reindeer hide, Lapp clothing has since been influenced by Scandinavian, Russian, and Central European styles. The bands in various shades of red and yellow, sewn to the collar, wrists, shoulders, and around the hems of the blue cloth jackets, for example, are of Viking extraction.

The origin of the gold and silver jewelry adorning the bride's bust is even more ancient, coming from distant Byzantium. The source of the pointed beret still remains mysterious. Symbolizing the four winds of the Arctic, it was prohibited in the second half of the nineteenth century, since it happened to remind a superstitious priest of the Devil's horns! The short-topped handmade boots known as *gallokak* are the only survival from the time when the Lapps dressed entirely in reindeer hide. Gathered tight by a hand-woven length of colored binding wrapped a few times round the ankle and topped by a multicolored wool pompon, these boots are specifically designed to keep the snow out. The toes pointing upwards

originally served to fix them beneath the strip of leather which at the time served as the only method of attaching the skis. Back then, the *gallokak* were worn barefoot and packed with a fibrous dried grass to provide insulation, absorb the sweat, and prevent frostbite.

The festive atmosphere at traditional wedding banquets that can last as long as three days is often heightened by numerous draughts of *aqua vitae* and by *joik*s improvised by the guests. Long condemned by the Church for its frequently scabrous content, the *joik* is a lyric poem chanted solo or *a capella*. Called by Turi "the art of recollecting others," through such ballads a Lapp can express strong feelings on any subject that comes to mind: a young girl's graceful mien, the huntsman's skill, the whistling of the wind, a blizzard, or snorting reindeer on the move. *Joik*s sung at weddings tell the story of the couple. Though they might exalt their virtues, they are by no means sparing of their defects and may evoke in ironical vein certain episodes from their past life: a fall from a snowmobile in his case, or abject defeat in a reindeer race for her. It is common too though to hear a *joik* in praise of the bride-to-be break out between two glasses of liquor. "Vaja vaja, nana nana, the bride is gentle indeed, and skillful, and amiable; vaja vaja, nana nana, she's the best girl on the mountain…"

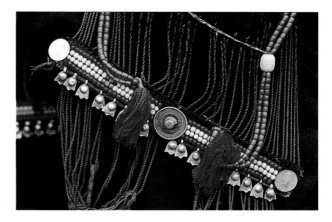

Coral is considered a good omen because of its color.

A wife's dowry always includes jewels of turquoise, "the gemstone that grants all our wishes" and that repels evil spirits.

CORAL AND TURQUOISE
The Tibetans

A strip of leopard (or tiger) skin fixed to a Tibetan man's jacket.

Reliquary in gold and silver.

RIGHT
A Tibetan bride.

FOLLOWING PAGES
The bridegroom's friends and his *nyempo* arrive at the bride's house.

For the nomadic shepherds of the vast, empty tracts of northern Tibet, rocks and rugged outcrops are home to all manner of evil spirits, while water, like a mirror, allows subterranean beings to spy on the world above, as if through an eye. Turquoise, though, is "a gem which can grant all your wishes."

A legend recounted by the Tibetan traveler Alexandra David-Neel tells of an enormous turquoise of a pure and extraordinarily bright blue. One day, a magician possessing supreme occult powers raised a water deity from the depths of Lake Kou Kou Nor Naga. The spirit presented him with a stone which, emerging suddenly from the depths and exposed for the first time to the sunlight, endowed its owner with the power to make wishes come true.

Today, not only in Tibet but throughout the Himalayas, turquoise is still regarded as a precious talisman because it is colored blue, the color of things divine. Since antiquity, it has been a gift worthy of sovereigns, divinities, and demons, and the Tibetans attribute many beneficial properties to it: worn in a ring, it protects the traveler; in an earring, it prevents the wearer being reincarnated as an ass; if it turns greenish, it shows the presence of hepatitis, which it can cure since it can reverse jaundice. It is thus a most precious gem, capable of absolving sin and dispersing malevolent beings.

Like coral and amber, turquoise is an important element in the dowry of all Tibetan wives. These three gemstones, which possess the colors of fire, earth, and air, have been an integral part of bridal hair ornament since time immemorial, and even Marco Polo referred to the inordinate Tibetan taste for coral. This valuable material, brought from the remote Mediterranean or the Andaman Sea, is regarded as more precious than gold. It is still said today that the wife who wears red coral will live happily ever after, since red is one of the colors of the five Buddhas and considered of good augur. In Western Tibet, it is also thought to aid menstrual flow.

Draped in thick yak-wool or fur-trimmed brocade tunics, Tibetan brides wear a profusion of priceless adornments and semi-precious stones attached to their braids. A cascade of amber, coral, and turquoises of all sizes, the hairpiece ornament called *pöden* reaches from the head to the waist. Among the nomads of Amdo and Kham, bridal hairstyles comprise one hundred and eight very fine plaits, without which a girl cannot enter into wedlock. An ancient chant has

When the husband alights from his horse, he is presented with a stool decorated with a swastika made out of barley grains to bring him good luck.

it that if a woman wears the braided hairstyle and the coral and amber *pöden* on her wedding day, it shows she is blessed with good-natured and loving parents. In certain areas of Kham, brides also wear a large amber ball surmounted by a branch of coral on the summit of their head. Elsewhere, they don a turquoise headband terminating in a larger stone that lies on the forehead as an ornament. In the Gyarongpa valleys that plunge from the high plateau to the plains of China, brides parade in a five-pointed headdress embellished with black and gold brocade.

In her dowry, every bride receives a *charma* (a broad silk belt about eight inches wide studded with silver nails called *borchen*), the *losar* (a finely chased silver medallion with a large half-moon fastener), and, among the nomads, a silver necklace with a hook, originally used to chain the milking-pail. It is an emblem of marriage referring to the bucket of milk which, according to custom, the mother of the bridegroom must present to her new daughter-in-law at the end of the ceremony.

Marriage is for the most part an affair arranged between the two families concerned and is preceded by exhaustive negotiations regarding the value of the dowry in terms of yak, *dri* (female yak), textiles, and wolf and leopard skins which the husband will have to bring to the couple's new home. The whole bargaining process is invariably carried out by an intermediary who is a member of neither family.

After the haggling, however, comes the drinking: *chang*, a fermented beverage based on barley, flows freely, and countless gifts, such as silk or woolen coverlets, are readily exchanged. The nomads call these gifts *nathag tak*, "the nose-rope," since, once accepted, the parents of the bride cannot back out of the marriage contract.

Tibetans are nearly all monogamists, though in the past marital relationships were somewhat more complex. Depending on the social class and the region, polygamy and polyandry were frequently encountered. Among the wealthy and the nobility, it was not rare for a man to take several wives, while among nomads and townsfolk, on the other hand, it was commonplace for a woman to marry several brothers from the same family, or else a father and son. The practice of polygamy could cite some illustrious examples: King Songtsen Gampo married the Chinese princess Wenchen and the Nepalese princess Brikuti, while Marpa, a Tantric grand master, had nine wives, who were essential to the ritual Wheel of Life known as *chakra*, used in the worship of Heruka. For its part, polyandry arose from the more practical desire to keep the family estate undivided. The wife was chosen by the elder brother, but, once the marriage was celebrated, his brothers automatically became joint husbands without further matrimonial rites being necessary. Even if rites and customs differ widely between the various regions of Tibet, weddings are not in general given sanction with a religious ceremony. Instead, there is a series of ritual farewells to the family divinities and the paternal roof, with the blessing of a lama. It is this holy man who, after careful consultation of the gods and the almanacs, selects the best date for the wedding.

On the day before the wedding, the suitor, accompanied by a few friends and an eminent personage from his own family known as the *nyenpo*, presents himself at the tent or house of his intended, bringing with him the horse on which he will carry her off. He is welcomed with *khata*, white ceremonial scarves that are exchanged in a show of mutual respect. After much drinking of *chang*, the group lodges with the family of the bride for three days before she leaves home with them. Among the Kham, it was traditional on this occasion for the groom to offer a female yak to his future mother-in-law, a present known as "the milk price" that is supposed to compensate for the loss of a daughter.

Dressed in all her finery and bedecked in jewels, the bride then sets out from her parents' house. She wears round her neck a *gao*, an engraved silver reliquary which contains an image of a divinity or of a great lama, designed to protect her from evil spirits at a time when she is highly vulnerable, since she is leaving the protection of the gods attached to the paternal home but has yet to gain the favor of those belonging to her husband's house.

With the nomads, custom demands that a girl be sent out to welcome the bride as she nears her new husband's dwelling place. Before taking her horse's bridle and leading her towards the house, the girl hands the young wife a pink scarf which she has to put over her mouth and ears. A red carpet (red being the color of marriage), which is also decorated with the swastika, is spread out on the ground to receive her as she dismounts. The bride crosses the threshold and is given a cup of yogurt: with the ring finger of her right hand she flicks a few drops skywards and invokes the protection of the Buddha and of the gods of the mountains, thus performing "the offering of the yogurt of the oath," the most deeply significant marriage ritual in all Tibet.

Pema, carrying a plate of offerings for the groom. A large container filled with *chang* and, in the background, a fox skin over a few bags of grain.

FOLLOWING PAGES
Bridal hairstyle made up of one hundred and eight braids adorned with a band of turquoises and coral (*right*). Girls still to be married wear their hair in two large plaits (*left*).

Silver, coral, amber, and turquoise
are all used to dress hair among
the nomads of Eastern Tibet.

FOLLOWING PAGES
The *nyenpo* and riders escorting
the groom.

Laterite powder mixed with water is used to draw the dotted crosses that accentuate the features.

Embroidered saddle-carpets.

LATERITE

The Tuaregs Kel-Air in Niger

Natural pigments: blusher for the cheeks and eye make-up for the Tuareg bride.

The Tuaregs are the princes of the desert. Of Arab origin, the name Tuareg apparently derives from Targa, an ancient name designating the site of modern-day Fezzan in Libya, whence these people reportedly came. Called the *Kel-tamacheq* (those who speak Tamacheq) or *Kel-tagelmoust* (those who wear a veil), the Tuaregs are of Berber stock. The name they are known by depends on the geographical area in which they live, but they share a common language. Nonetheless, they are generally known as "Men of Blue" because of the indigo stain left on their skin by the *tagelmoust*, a light veil around twenty feet long which fathers give their young sons when they reach adulthood at the age of eighteen. Since the remote past, the dye which darkens their skin has been their emblem. Indeed, indigo, a rare and very expensive commodity in the desert, has become a sign of Tuareg prosperity.

Although they are bound by a common culture, Tuaregs observe differing matrimonial customs according to their rank and the region over which they roam. Marriage was formerly an affair arranged between the respective parents, with girls often being wed when hardly more than children. A prepubescent young girl might be led to her betrothed's encampment and force-fed milk to give her a fully nubile appearance, so that marriages were consummated prematurely. Such customs have long since been abandoned, and today marriage is a matter of choice in which the engaged couple is actively involved. Even if marriage still takes place mainly within the clan, the woman reserves the right to refuse an applicant.

Among the Tuaregs of Niger, a boy trying to woo the girl of his choice has first to sneak at night into the tent in which she sleeps with her parents and tickle her ear until she wakes up. If the girl covers her head with the sheet, his suit has been summarily rejected; if, on the other hand, she takes her mat and moves a little away from her parents, the nocturnal meeting is transformed into a kind of verbal sparring-match, the young man being expected to solve all the riddles his sweetheart murmurs into his ear. If he succeeds in solving these puzzles, he is well on the way to becoming the young girl's beau and will be able to display in public a talisman or pendant that she has given to him. Marriage is preceded by an agreement designed to determine the exact amount of dowry, "the bride-price," or *taggalt* in Tamacheq.

Among the Tuaregs, it is the groom who pays a dowry for the woman he intends to marry—goods which become the exclusive property of his wife following the wedding. Most often this consists of camels and goats, sometimes with two silver bracelets, a blanket, or a couple of pairs of leather sandals. For its part, the bride's family has to cover the expenses of the ceremony and the trousseau, including a tent with all its furnishings such as blankets and carpets, which the young wife will take with her on the day of *azalay*, the rite which marks the spouses' change of residence and the start of their life together as a family.

The marriage is signed and sealed by the two families before the *marabout*, who recites a *sura* from the Qur'an to ensure the union is granted divine protection. It takes place in the fiancée's home encampment during a time of full moon, an auspicious time of the month that ensures the young couple good fortune (*baraka*). The ceremony itself usually stretches over several days, during which the bride takes herself off to a tent a little outside the main camp. It has been specially erected by the women at a site that has first been purified by the sacrifice of a goat. The tent protects the bride from the fierce sun and keeps the inquisitive at bay. Inside, the floor is covered with several layers of carpet and blankets, on which stands the great bed where the marriage is to be consummated. The sides of the tent are hung with some of the equipment essential to nomadic life, including the *ahalu*, a sharp, iron-tipped tool used by women to dig the holes to fix the tent in place. In a Tuareg marriage the *ahalu* symbolizes security for the female and fulfills the same role as the sword, or *takuba*, for a man. The *ahalu* and the *takuba*, both made out of metal, are regarded as offering stalwart defense against the *djinn*, an important advantage, since newly-weds are considered particularly vulnerable to the attacks from these malevolent spirits during the marriage ceremony. Normally, the *ahalu* is presented by the blacksmith, a member of the community that no family would ever forget to invite to the nuptials. Held in great regard by the Tuaregs, these farriers (*inaden*) are believed to possess occult powers because of their ability to work metals—in particular silver, blessed by the Prophet, and iron, supposed to repel a malfeasant spirit known as Kel-Essuf.

It is the blacksmith's wife, a woman well versed in the secrets of the plants and rocks of the desert, who prepares the fiancée's make-up in the privacy of the bridal tent: She uses *tamagsoit* (a red clay paste) to soften the skin, an aromatic cream to scent and moisturize the hair before it is plaited into fine braids, a mash of flowers and grass to stain the face yellow, and laterite powder mixed with water, with which she draws the pale red vertical crosses on the bride's face. Natural pigments or modern make-up materials are used to decorate the cheeks of the bride with tiny pastel-colored dots resembling half-open petals. Finally the feet and hands of the young couple are hennaed as a symbol of both purity and fertility.

The guests arrive in all their finery—the women covered in jewels, seated on asses on colorful blankets and surrounded by richly decorated leather cushions, the men on camelback, their faces swathed in *tagelmoust*s and adorned in silver amulet-chains.

The culmination of the wedding festivities is the *ilugan*, a love parade in which the women play the *tende*, a drum, to whose beat the men encourage the camels—harnessed for the occasion with ceremonial saddles—to dance. Arranged in a circular huddle, the women bang on their tam-tams, while the men circle round them on camels at a rhythmic amble. Some way off, the groom, a motionless, silent witness to the scene, waits until the sun goes down before joining his new wife.

RIGHT AND FOLLOWING PAGES
Inside the bridal tent the women chat, apply their make-up, and attend to the preparation of the bride.

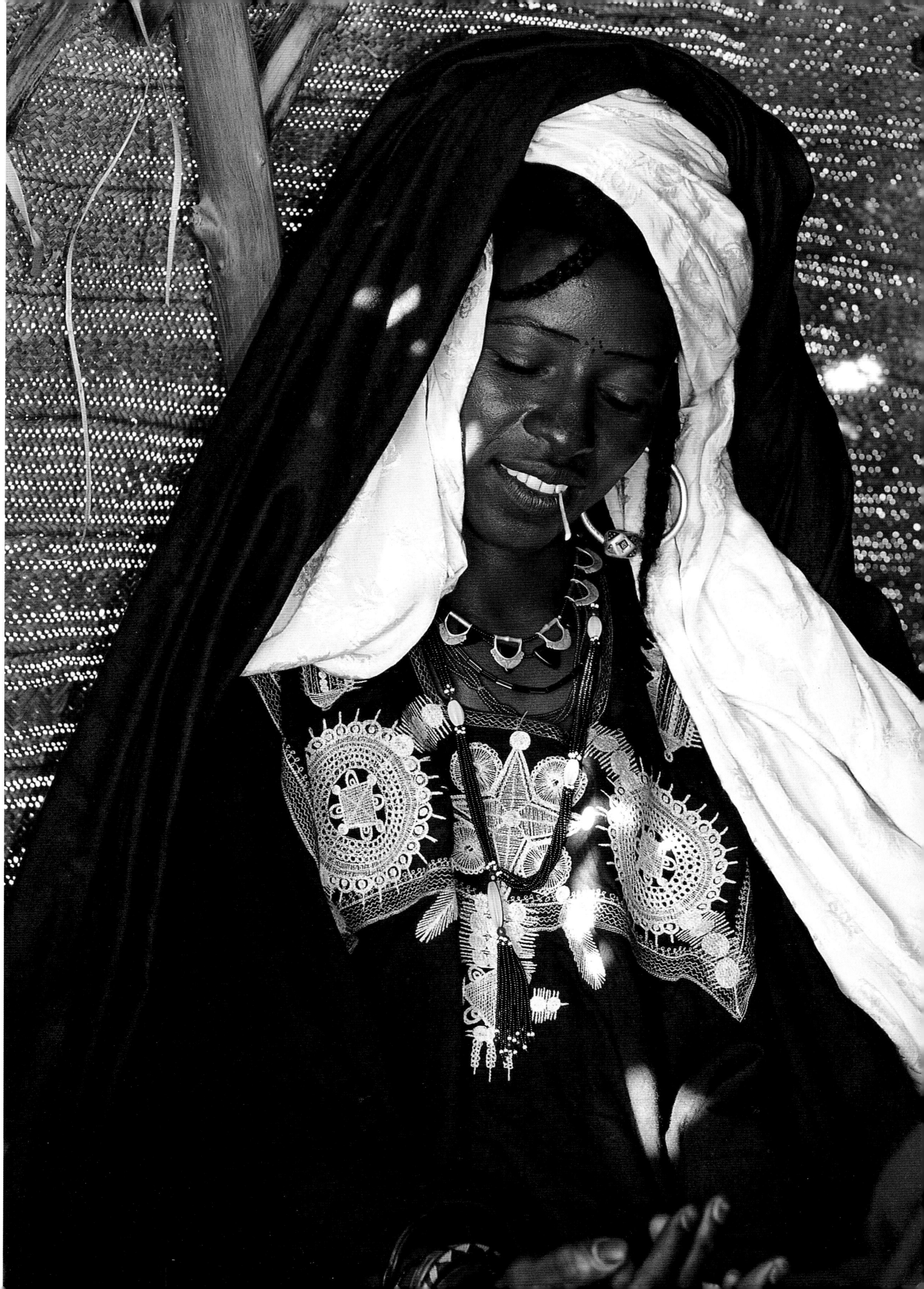

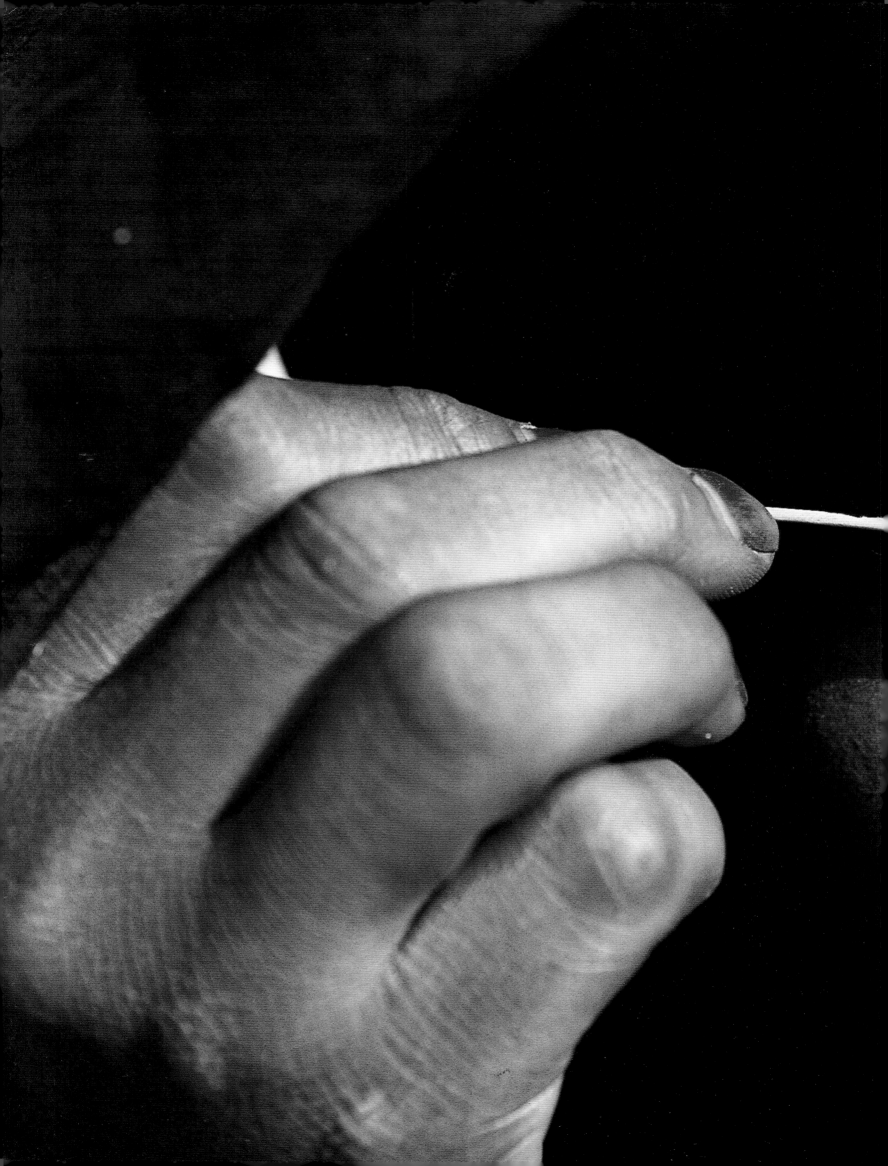

Preparing and applying henna, a symbol of
purity and fertility, while the blacksmith's
wife plaits the bride's hair into fine braids.

FOLLOWING PAGES
Woman playing the *tende* and, in the
background, a camel parade at the festival
of *ilugan*.

Embroidery representing a visit from the sukaabe.

Preparation of *pura*, a pigment extracted from an ochre shard found in *kori* (dry riverbeds) in the vicinity of In Gall.

OCHRE

The Peulh Bororos of Niger

Gris-gris and talismans used to increase *sukaabe* charm.

A calabash filled with milk that accompanies the endogamous marriage vows (*koobgal*), celebrated at the *worso*.

Among the Peulh Bororos of Niger, the word *togu* denotes a blend of charm and seduction that has to come from the heart—a particular way of smiling, of speaking. It is their cordiality, kindness, elegance of manner, and voice which make the Bororo people so alluring. Young people are taught the arts of seduction at the *daddo*, a kind of school in which they are initiated into the ways of love. Here, boys and girls alike, under the watchful eye of their elders, are free to try out all sorts of beguiling ploys. Only then can they be united to a partner whom their families have chosen for them when they were little children.

The Bororos believe that anyone who possesses *togu*—be they male or female—will never be truly lonely. Its charm will guarantee not only the conquest of a loved one but the esteem and benevolence of the whole community as well. With patience and determination, the young Bororos learn all the tricks and wiles of this seductive art, from conversation to mastery over the body. A languishing glance, a solicitous gesture, a bright smile: these are the surest weapons in the arsenal of any *sukaabe* (or young man), that he deploys to attract and subdue his *surbaabe*—young woman. Physical beauty and charm are paramount qualities for the Bororos, particularly for the menfolk. Bororo males spend more time and care on their make-up and dress than their female counterparts. To enhance his *togu* and increase his appeal to the opposite sex, a Bororo man is ready even to resort to philters and magic potions.

Every time we ran into Fedu leading his cattle to the watering-hole, we were forcibly struck by the elegance and easy distinction of every gesture he made. He seemed to be endowed with a grace like that of the figures in the prehistoric paintings decorating the caves of Tassili. In these images, dating from thousands of years before Christ, long-haired, slim men are shown standing next to dappled oxen with huge lyre-shaped horns.

The presumed creators of these mysterious cave paintings, the Bororos, are one of the most ancient peoples in all Africa. According to a legend recorded by Hampatè Ba, they are supposed to have arrived in Africa from a distant Orient land, the mythical country of Heli and Yoyo, lying beyond an immense stretch of water. One theory has it that they are of Judeo-Syrian origin and

Young men (*sukaabe*) apply red ochre (*pulla*)
and yellow ochre (*pura*) make-up as they
prepare for the *yake* in the shade of a tent
or under a tree.

A vertical line running from the forehead to the chin underscores the pure lines of the profile.

FOLLOWING PAGES
Lips painted black with coal brings out the whiteness of their teeth.
In the *yake* dance, young *sukaabe* rival one another in the seductive arts.

that they mixed with indigenous African peoples during three successive waves of migration. Another hypothesis makes them of Nilotic origin and speculates that they arrived in the central Sahara by way of Tibesti, Tassili, Hoggar, and the Iforas Adrar. Wherever they came from in the distant past, the present-day homeland of the Bororos is the Sahel, the endless savanna in the southern Sahara that extends from Senegal to Niger and Chad. It is a tough, arid terrain which, especially during periods of drought, demands of its inhabitants unimaginable moral strength and will to survive. Dispensing with huts and tents, the Bororos live in total symbiosis with their zebu herds, sleeping under the stars and migrating freely wherever nature calls the animals. They are the only members of the Peulh group to have preserved these traditions and their love of freedom. Following the conversion to Islam of the Fulbe peoples, they became a nomadic pagan minority, scorned by sedentary Peulh communities and other local ethnic groups, who regard them even today as a lawless and heathen people. Even their local name testifies to this widespread contempt. It would seem that "*Wodaabe*" means either the "secluded," or, according to other sources, the "taboo" people.

Fedu and two companions had lain down in the shade of a "palaver tree" (in this case an acacia) from whose branches hang swords, goatskin satchels, large conical caps, make-up materials, and other personal ornaments—in short, everything a shepherd needs to turn him into an alluring and handsome prince ready to conquer with come-hither looks and beguiling smiles the heart of any woman. The Wodaabe are a people of great creativity, which they express through make-up, dance, and in a taste for all forms of physical adornment. They are past masters in the arts of face-painting, through which they give free rein to an innate aesthetic sense, creating designs that, though principally intended to attract members of the opposite sex, are little short of masterpieces of pictorial art.

To highlight the radiance and the smooth tones of his complexion, Fedu paints his face with *pura*, a yellow pigment extracted from shards of ochre that he had collected in the dried-out *kori* near the In Gall oasis during his travels. To bring out the best in his flawless profile, he draws a vertical line from the middle of the forehead to the base of the chin with some egg-white *karmari*, a paste purchased at the market at Tahoua. Smearing the ochre foundation over his face, he then emphasizes the whites of his eyes by lining them with kohl, while blackening his lips with coal to accentuate the contrast with his gleaming teeth. Fedu then carefully rolls a traditional white turban around his head, on which he affixes a band of blue fabric containing his talismans. The Bororo firmly believes in the power of these talismans, which are prepared using formulae handed down from father to son, and constitute part of the bloodline's heritage.

Bororos know well the secrets of the soil and tree-bark from which they take pigments to make the skin shine. They also extract perfumes from certain leaves and resins to increase *togu* and prepare potions or decoctions to improve their chances in the war of seduction. The men also know how to prepare an ointment from the fruit of the *barkehi*, the tree of good fortune, to protect them from the evil eye. Prior to dancing the *yake*—a dance of seduction whose sole goal is to enchant the young women—they even exploit the power of the chameleon by spreading over their face a mixture of water and dust obtained from the desiccated body of the animal. Fedu, with his chest draped in *gris-gris* and an ostrich feather threaded through his turban, prepares to exhibit his stamina as well as his *togu* at the *yake*.

To attract the young *surbaabe*, Bororo men roll their eyes, grin broadly and make sounds imitating kisses.

It was now the end of the rainy season. More than a thousand Wodaabe of the Bikorawa lineage had arranged to meet in the region around Tamaya for the *worso*, the annual gathering at which births and marriages are celebrated. In the space of a single afternoon, the plain that heavy rain had carpeted with grass was filled with nomads. They had all returned from the long trek to northern Niger where their herds had been on the "salty cure" to build up the energy necessary to face the deprivations of a yet another dry season.

While the zebu grazed obliviously, the men met up and prepared for the festival devoted to beauty and seduction. These nomadic peoples look forward for months to great annual gatherings such as the *worso* and *geerewol*. The first provides an opportunity for the members of the same bloodline to exchange news, celebrate births, and arrange marriages within the group known as *koobgal*; at the second, new alliances are forged and marriages arranged with members of other lineages.

The Wodaabe become engaged at birth, regarding marriage with members of the same clan as a means of keeping the family and its property together. In this way they preserve their ethnic purity but at the same time they avoid the risks of degeneration in their stock by limiting marriage to that between kin of the fourth degree of relationship. Every promise of marriage is accompanied by a gift of money and water-bottles full of milk which the boy's family presents to the girl's as a token of the couple's engagement.

During the *worso*, the spouses' families seal the wedding agreement by sacrificing a bull, whereupon the women start to chant: "He's cut its throat—he's married off his son." The flesh of the animal, which the Wodaabe call the "bull of *koobgal* marriage," is shared out according to a ritualized symbolic system that reserves tripe and intestines, symbols of fruitfulness, for the women, the men getting the testicles, representing procreation, and the old men the animal's hooves. From this point on, the engaged couple is designated by the term *kore* or "spouses." The two young people must observe an attitude of reserve and are forbidden to speak to one other or call each other by their name.

In addition to endogamous unions dictated by family considerations, the Bororos also have another form of marriage called *teegal*, a kind of "free love" which allows a woman unhappy in wedlock to elope with a man belonging to another clan. These informal unions are more expeditious affairs than *koobgal*s. Unbeknownst to her family, the woman simply follows the man she has chosen to his resident camp. There their union is speedily celebrated by the sacrifice of an animal before the legal husband realizes the woman has escaped.

During the *geerewol*, a week-long gathering named for the dance that takes place there, the men compete in charm and beauty in a tournament that alternates *yake*, the dance of seduction, with *geerewol*, the dance of beauty. Its purpose is to attract women who have decided to leave their husband and find another among the members of another kinship group.

Fedu was getting ready to do his level best at the first bout, the *yake*, which concentrates on charm and personality. With a group of friends, he set to, training himself to roll his eyes and even getting them to point in different directions. He knew that the women judging him against his peers set great store by such skills, and he especially hoped to impress Jika, a girl with gazelle-like eyes belonging to the Kasasawa line. Fedu was a paragon of Wodaabe beauty: lithe, sinewy body, broad forehead, smooth complexion, and an oval face that emphasized his straight nose, bright eyes, and delicate lips. The Peulh attach such importance to physical beauty that mothers take particular care over the body of their new-born offspring: they massage the skull, moulding its original form and softening the profile, and twist the arms, legs, and nose in the hope that the baby acquires a physique conforming to the Peulh aesthetic canon.

The time for dancing had at last arrived. Hand in hand, Fedu and other *sukaabe*s of his line made their way to the space set aside for the *yake*. Around fifty young men belonging to the Bikorawa and Kasasawa lineages, ranging in age from fifteen to thirty-five, gathered on a line running from north to south, and, as instructed by their respective *samri* (the youngsters' traditional mentors) turned to face the west. Under the watchful eye of Hasan—a Wodaabe man of around forty, the overseer of the *sukaabe*s of the Bikorawa line—Fedu and his friends started to dance. They first bent their knees as gracefully as they could before quickly stretching up on tiptoe; they then lifted their arms decorated with goatskin bracelets, simultaneously lowering their head and making the ostrich feathers bob up and down in time.

The youths exploited every weapon of seduction, opening their eyes wide, grinning broadly to bring out the whiteness of their teeth, while their lips quivered imperceptibly, emitting a smacking sound like a kiss. Indifferent to heat and dust, the Bororo youths danced on for hours under the unremitting sun, giving no sign of flagging or tiring, thereby proving to everyone present not only their great charm but also their strength and endurance.

During the *geerewol*, women unhappy in their present marriage may acquire a new husband from a different clan.

FOLLOWING PAGES
Sukaabe of the same bloodline dancing the *ruume* together.

Seated in a group in front of the long line of *sukaabe*s, the women pass a critical eye over the proceedings, sparing no-one with their comments. Among them, Jika cast a few timid glances in Fedu's direction in response to the discreet signs he had addressed to her. Every now and again, to shouts of admiration from the assembly, the *samri* would touch a dancer's shoulder with the point of his sword to indicate he had caught the eye of one of the girls, and would urge him to step out of line.

If the *yake* sees the Bororo youths competing for attractiveness, the *ruume* has them dancing together in a single round to celebrate the unity of the community. A dance of welcome at daytime, but one of seduction at night, a *ruume* performed by the *sukaabe*s of the same lineage represents a paean of love to a beautiful girl.

Fedu joined the circle with some other dancers. To the beat of a slow, monotone chant and accompanied by handclaps from the *sukaabe*s, the dancers moved off with little steps, forming a ring that rotated in an anti-clockwise direction. In the gloom, one could spot huddles of girls attracted by the melody. Her face partially hidden behind her embroidered veil, Jika gazed on Fedu, who, conscious of her attention, danced with still greater enthusiasm. Jika passed by him cautiously, lightly fingering his tunic and wandered off into the bush. Equally discreetly, Fedu left the circle of men, and disappeared into the darkness.

Henna, "the powder of paradise," safeguards the bride from spells and maledictions.

El-jawhar, a pearl adornment which has lent its name to the attire of the wives of Fez.

HENNA AND PEARLS

The Fassi, Morocco

Shining pearls are regarded as offering protection against the evil eye.

A *neggafa* preparing the table for the henna ceremony.

FOLLOWING PAGES
Melika seated on the *glissa* between the *neggafa* and her ululating assistants.

El-*jawhar*, the "dress of pearls," is the name of the traditional bridal costume in Fez. Celebrated by poets as the solidified tears of sea nymphs, and in ancient Arab texts long associated with Paradise, pearls form a predominant element in Fassi wedding adornments. Their shiny surface is considered a formidable defense against the evil eye, and so the vital parts of the bride's body, the head and chest, are literally covered in them; a twist of irregular pearls alternating with synthetic emeralds, known as *selta*, adorn the hairline; two coarse-net ribbons made of minuscule freshwater pearls, *zrair*, frame the face; and a drape of baroque pearls held by gold and green gemstone tie-backs covers the upper bust.

The choice of the bride's apparel and personal adornments, as well as the rituals designed to combat malevolent spirits during the delicate transition period between maidenhood and conjugal life, are entrusted to a *neggafa*—a "matchmaker" or "wedding planner" believed to possess magic powers. For over two centuries these women have been appointed by the brides' families to oversee the immensely complex nuptial ceremonials laid down by Moroccan tradition. If their time-honored role as instructors in sexual education is today obsolete, they remain professionals in all matters matrimonial and are responsible for the wedding preparations, able to offer the families concerned an extensive range of "services" from dress and jewelry hire to arrangements for the reception.

We are in the middle of the *medina*, a close-knit tangle of tumbledown houses crisscrossed by an inextricable maze of alleyways, at the house of the most celebrated and esteemed *neggafa* in all of Fez—or perhaps in all Morocco. As she opens the door, we see an imposing-looking woman, her dark-skinned face framed by the scarf wrapped around her head.

In a huge room lined in blue and white wall tiles, her assistants, addressing her respectfully as *maalma*, "Mistress," now and again ask for advice on some aspect or other of the wedding dress for Melika, the latest, very young bride-to-be. Brocade caftans with floral motifs, matching *djellaba*s with gossamer pastel-colored silk veils (*izar*), necklaces, belts, broaches, earrings: everything is gradually taken out of the many wardrobes and packed into two large suitcases.

"There was a time," the *neggafa* tells us, flicking through a photo album that also serves as a catalog itemizing the various outfits she supplies, "when the festivities would last a whole week. The *neggafa* herself instructed the bride-to-be in all aspects of conjugal life and would also offer a personal guarantee as to the girl's virginity. She would prepare the bridal chamber and, for seven evenings preceding the wedding itself, would accompany the girl to the *hammam* for ritual purification." The *neggafa* nostalgically recounted a time when the intimate atmosphere of the cubicles at the *hammam*, lit by a few candles, was filled with invocations to the Prophet and heavy with the scent of incense, amber, and sandalwood. Her eyes lit up as she told of those far-off days, and we pictured her measuring a young bride's feet so that the fiancé could have slippers made for her, or else arranging pearls around some young girl's face and instructing her in the secrets of the bed-chamber.

The hectic rhythm of modern life has today curtailed festivities that now last only a weekend. It has also reduced the size of the wardrobe which the bride has to wear for her guests. Originally, no fewer than seven outfits were called for, but today there are never more than five, and sometimes there are only three, depending on the family's means.

On the eve of the reception, a small group of women gathers at Melika's home to apply the henna. It is a cheerful but strictly private occasion from which men are traditionally excluded. Melika's entrance is heralded by a chorus of *zgharit*, the joyous ululation mentioned by Herodotus. She wears a caftan of green silk—the color of wealth—whose sleeves are tied back by a thin chain of engraved gold cylinders known as *tkhmel*; the *lebba*, a diamond-shaped piece comprising rows of silver gilt drops set with zircons and emeralds, covers her bust. Like the pearl necklace, it is

thought to be a talisman that protects against demonic possession and evil spells. So that every-one can have a chance of admiring her, Melika sits high up on a *glissa* covered with a bolt of green velvet. To protect the young girl from envious eyes, the *neggafa* advances and, pretending to plump up the cushions, secretly slips under one of the seven mattresses making up the *glissa* a lit-tle cloth bag embroidered in cross-stitch containing *chabba* (crystal), *oud* (sandalwood), and *sharghina* (a plant with prophylactic powers).

In fact, the number seven, the symbol of a complete cycle, recurs throughout the nuptials: the seven days of feasting; the seven mattresses comprising the *glissa* at the henna ceremony; the seven evenings spent at the *hammam*, the seven buckets of water sprinkled over the fiancée's body, and the seven wedding garments worn by the bride during the celebrations.

On a small table in the middle of the room, a length of green tulle with a few verses from the Qur'an embroidered on it in gold thread safeguard the case containing the make-up from anyone intent on harming the bride. The salver of henna, the kohl for Melika's eyes, the flasks of rosewa-ter and orange-flower water, the incense, the sugar-loaves, and the sprigs of mint and marjoram are all prepared with the greatest respect for tradition.

"The beauty and future happiness of a bride," the *neggafa* goes on, "makes her particularly vul-nerable. Hence every stage of the ceremony must be placed under divine protection and take place at the most propitious time possible. The milk, honey, sugar-loaves, rosewater, orange-flower water, and the color green—which refers to Paradise and which is so frequently used in our wed-ding dresses—are all symbols of purity, gentleness, prosperity, and happiness." Taking Melika's hand in her own, Fatma, a henna artiste—in fact a sculptress, since this is the meaning of the Arabic

A *neqqasha* applying henna to Melika's hands.

FOLLOWING PAGES
Sandalwood, *sharghina*, and *chabba* burning in a small silver brazier in order to protect the bride against evil intent.

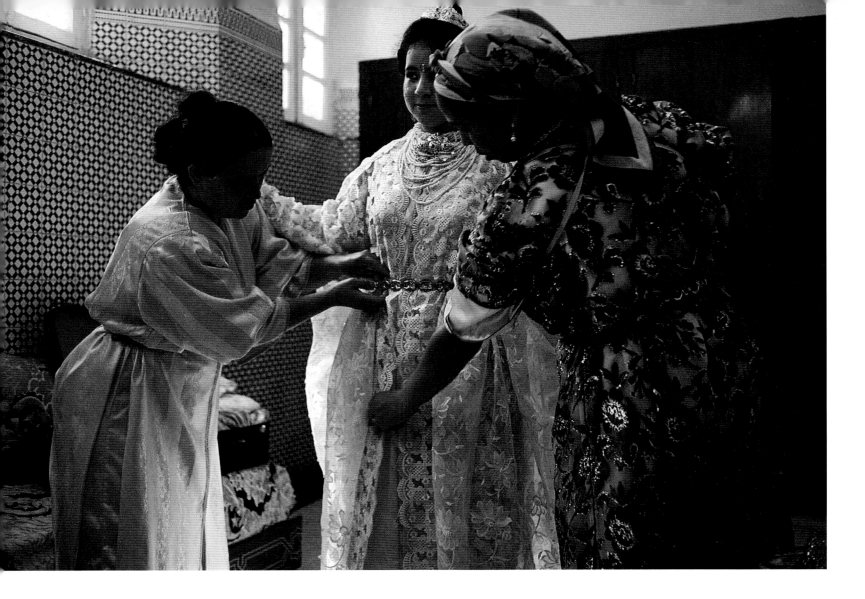

neqqasha—lists the antiseptic and purifying proprieties of *Lawsonia inermis*, a plant cultivated in the oases of southern Morocco, from which henna is extracted.

"Bodily extremities are especially susceptible," Fatma explains, playing out a henna arabesque freehand over Melika's fingers. "They allow the demons and the evil eye a way in to get at the vital parts. Applied to the hands and feet, henna erects a barrier that protects the bride from all known malevolent influences." Henna is said to come from Paradise. Common throughout the Islamic world, for centuries it has played a prophylactic and propitiatory role in Moroccan nuptials. Its Arab name *al hinna* sounds like words such as *hnana* (tenderness) and *hna* (peace) and recalls past links with the virtues of marriage. "Long ago," the *neggafa* again informs us, "the night of henna—as the ceremony preceding the wedding is known—was performed according to a highly complex ceremony. Henna had to be prepared by seven *mezwarat* (first wives) who pound it in a mortar with lavender, cloves, saffron, and myrtle."

The air was saturated with perfume: alum (*shebba*), *Peganum harmala*, sandalwood, and *sharghina*, burnt on a small silver brazier once again to protect the newly-wed from evil intentions. The *neqqasha* washes the dark, dry paste, while the *neggafa* grabs Melika's hand. She is eager to read in the ochre stain the henna has deposited on the skin indications as to the young girl's character. Her expression lightens: the network of interlocking arabesques is of a full, bright hue, a sure sign of a pure and generous spirit. The *maalma*, in a gesture at once of well-wishing and dismissal, douses rosewater over Melika and all the other women.

If the henna ceremony takes place on Friday, Saturday is traditionally set aside for the wedding reception itself. The key event of the evening is of course the appearance of the bride. In

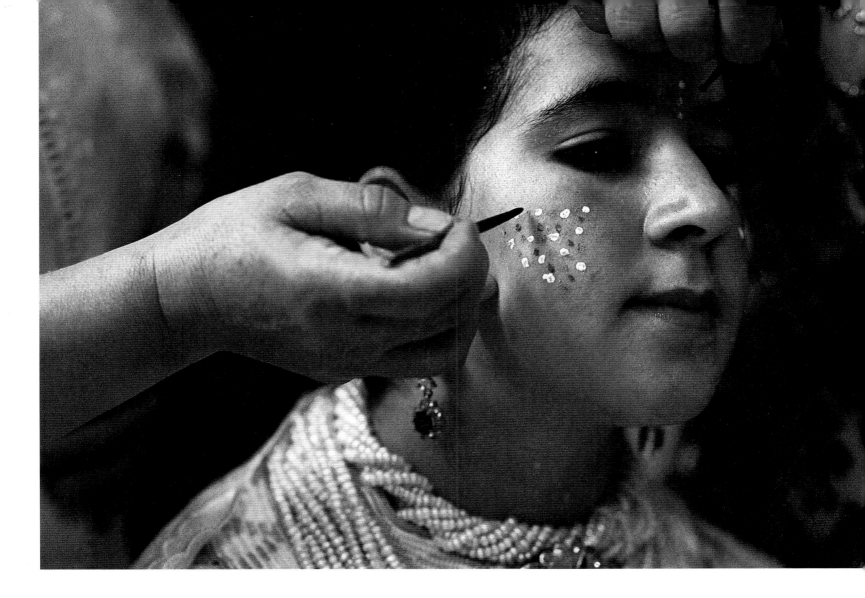

accordance with the custom, young Melika appears to the guests hoisted up on an *ammaria*, a modern version of a sedan-chair, in which in former times the *neggafa*s would carry the fiancée to the bridegroom's house. Preceded by her groom, who is dressed in a white *djellaba* and sports a purple fez, Melika enters, enclosed in a kind of tabernacle draped in green velvet embellished with silver-thread embroidery, and bobbing up and down on the shoulders of her four *neggafa*s. So begins a long night punctuated by an occasional apparition from the new bride, each time wearing a different outfit comprising sumptuous garments and jewelry that are intended to draw the admiration and the applause of the assembled guests.

The summer heat is oppressive, but there is no let-up for the *neggafa*s. There is always something that needs doing: a pin to stick in here, an eyebrow to line there, or a cheek that requires making-up with a multitude of little white and blue circles or triangles.

It is in fact the traditional nature of Fez, the most conservative town in Morocco, that maintains, in the teeth of the inevitable influence of the modern world, the more typical aspects of the nuptial ceremony. For example, the *fatiha*—or prayer that every Muslim must address to Allah—is still recited jointly by the two families at the mosque so as to place the future union under divine protection. The marriage is ratified and made legally binding before a registrar, but it is the traditional *dawra*, the ritual that publicly seals the union of the newly-weds in the presence of all the guests, which is the crucial moment. For the *dawra*, and for the *dawra* only, Melika has to wear the *jawhar*, the pearl garment for which brides in Fez have become renowned. The *neggafa*s help her to slip on the heavy pink brocade caftan with a floral pattern. They then put on her protective padded neckerchief and ensconce her in a thick plastron made of velvet-faced cardboard onto

The *neggafa* prepares the wedding garments during the auspicious period of Ramadan. The pearls are bought during a pilgrimage to Mecca.

Melika being dressed in an outfit of pearls with gold and silk brocade, the name of which, *khirb*, alludes to the financial outlay it requires of the family.

which the wedding *lebba*, with its five rows of openwork pendants, is fixed. The eldest assistant, or *saanaa*, winds a pair of pearl necklaces around her neck and completes her headdress with the *nowassi*, two strips of gold-embroidered and pearl-studded cloth that hang down to the waist. The adornments that make up the pearl wardrobe are prepared during the preceding Ramadan by the *neggafa*. Then, by fasting and prayer, they call divine blessing on the bride wearing them.

In her *jawhar*, Melika looks nothing like the modern young woman whom we had previously met. She has become an icon from another age, a bride from the splendor of Pharaonic times. Seated cross-legged on the *mida*, her face ringed by pearls and crowned by a silver-gilt diadem, her body totally swamped in the red and white silk brocade *khirb* with its weft of gold, Melika seems to resemble nothing more than a sphinx.

Amidst cries of admiration, she is hoisted onto the shoulders of four *neggafa* and carried off in procession. Meanwhile, on another *mida,* the husband also perches on the shoulders of four male porters. The room is filled with music and the excitement reaches fever pitch. Slowly, the *neggafa*s and the porters move the two *mida*s closer together. As stipulated by *dawra* tradition, it is the groom who leans out to kiss his bride on the forehead, the place where the *khit el-rih* or "thread of the wind" pendant hangs. Visibly satisfied, the *maalma* summons her attendants with a curt gesture and Melika is whisked away once more, leaving her guests.

The reception draws to a close. Back in the dressing chamber, the *neggafa* gives everyone leave and asks to be left alone with the bride. Is it to say her farewells? Or is she perhaps giving some advice, like the *neggafa*s of old? We never had a chance to find out.

RIGHT
Melika is carried on an *ammaria* draped in embroidered velvet.

ABOVE AND FOLLOWING PAGES
The bride and groom are carried shoulder-high on *mida*s and bounced up and down during the *dawra*.

The sheer amount of gold worn by Minangkabau couples refers back to the time when Sumatra was known as the Isle of Gold.

Headgear in the shape of buffalo horns is an emblem of the position occupied by women in the matriarchal society of Minangkabaus.

GOLD
The Minangkabaus, Indonesia

Jewelry belongs to the maternal clan and it is returned after the wedding.

Levina Rosa and Yulfariki Abdul
Aziz in Tanah Datar costume on
the day of the *adat* ceremony.

Hidden behind all the women fussing over her and putting the finishing touches to her gold-threaded headcloth, the *takuluak*, Levina Rosa was hardly visible. Like a buffalo horn in shape, the *takuluak* symbolizes the importance of women and their descendants in the matrilinear society of the Minangkabaus. Opening a trunk, the grandmother, the most powerful member of the family, took out a head ornament made of gold-leafed and inlaid wood, also in the shape of a pair of buffalo horns, and placed it on her granddaughter's head. Traditionally worn by the women of her lineage on their wedding day for more than two centuries, the gilt wood *takuluak emas* is a family treasure, an heirloom passed down from mother to daughter.

Levina Rosa, daughter of one of the two chiefs of the Kutiangiri clan from Lintau, comes from the Tanah Datar district (or *luah*), the oldest center of Minangkabau population on Sumatra, an island known since the time of Ptolemy as "Yavadvipa"—the Isle of Gold. According to legend, the Minangkabaus descend from Alexander the Great; ethnological research, however, indicates that they originated in southern China.

At all events, the Minangkabaus—a name that signifies "victorious buffalo"—initially settled on the slopes of Mount Merapi, a region that was rich in gold mines. Located on the crossroads between India and China, and since Antiquity famous for the quality of its gold, Sumatra enjoyed considerable profit from its flourishing trade in precious metals until the Dutch colonial period. Dugouts laden with gold descended the rivers from the Tanah Datar to the east coast and returned filled with silk and other goods from China and India. Gold was so important in the economy of the Minangkabau kingdoms that their king, Adity Awarman, a prince who had arrived on the island in the fourteenth century, adopted the title "Suwarnadwipa," or "Lord of the Land of Gold."

A throwback to the splendor of the court at Pagarruyung—the former Minangkabau capital—gold is still present today in the costumes and decorations of Sumatran wedding ceremonies. Bracelets, necklaces, belts, and pins of solid or rolled gold are not only signs of wealth: personal adornment also forms an integral part of *adat*, the set of rules applying to all fields of behavior—including the selection of clothes and jewelry worn at weddings—that has governed the Minangkabaus from time immemorial.

A ceremonial fabric with a gold yarn weft, the *songket*, is wrapped round Levina Rosa's hips like a sarong. It is decorated with four golden bands with friezes representing the four virtues required of a Minangkabau woman: serenity, wisdom, thrift, and the ability to manage the house

Levina Rosa dressing and donning the family jewels for the *adat* ceremony. On her head, an ancient and very rare gilt-wood *takuluak emas*. Around her neck are gold and Tibetan coral necklaces dating from the nineteenth century.

and the family property, since in the Minangkabaus' matrilinear system, land belongs to the women and is handed down from mother to daughter.

The weavers of Pandai Sikek, a village in the vicinity of Bukkitinggi, even call the *songket* the "skin of *adat*." Indeed, the ornamental motifs figuring on the bridal sarong amount to an intensive course in *adat*, a code based on Nature from which the Minangkabaus draw the fundamental precepts ruling their lives: "Nature is our Guide," runs an old *adat* saying that Levina Rosa's mother quoted.

"Bamboo," she went on, pointing to an isosceles triangle we could make out on the fabric, "symbolizes the three men entrusted with safeguarding our culture: the *pangulu*, the head of clan who enforces the *adat*; the *ulama*, the spiritual head who safeguards Islamic principles, and the *cadiak pandai*, the wise elders who decide on the future of our village. *Itiak pulang patang*," she added, running her finger over serried ranks of oblique S-shapes, "represents the ducks returning to the house late in the afternoon. They swim in the ponds, eat in the paddy-fields, but, come evening, they all waddle home, beak to tail. It is much the same with the Minangkabaus. Even if they are far away, they should never forget their hearth and home."

Trussed up in her *songket* and tunic of black velvet—the color of her clan—Levina Rosa found it hard to move. Despite hours of toil, the busying women never quite seemed satisfied with what they had done and carried on discussing everything down to the last detail. Should the young woman wear this or that set of bracelets? Should the gold necklaces and coral from Tibet be joined by a gold filigree pendant reminiscent of the *rumah adat*, the Minang houses

with their buffalo-horn shaped roofs? They might have gone on in the same vein for hours had not one of Levina's relatives knocked at the door to announce that it was time to set off for the groom's house. While a messenger went on before, carrying the copper *cerano* containing the ingredients for chewing-betel, Levina Rosa made her way to the house of Abdul Aziz, escorted by her four young bridesmaids, known as *sumandan*. A procession of women followed this first group, carrying plates laden with food. Amongst other things was a baked fish, symbol of the unbreakable bonds that a marriage forges between the two families. Levina Rosa was welcomed by a deluge of yellow tamaris rice as a token of blessing.

Levina Rosa was seated atop a pile of cushions and embroidered coverlets on the *palaminan*, the bridal podium erected within the *rumah adat* where the newlyweds accept the congratulations of their guests. As Minang tradition demands, following a religious ceremony, which makes the marriage legally binding, the couple go on to the groom's residence for an *adat* rite which allows members of the two families to get to know each other better and so consolidate the newly forged matrimonial links between the two clans. Abdul Aziz and Levina Rosa remained seated motionless for hours on end while before them representatives of the various clans engaged in a kind of a verbal tournament, firing off poetical salvoes, or *pantum pantum*.

One guest started up: "The bride and the groom sit side by side like the sun and the moon. The guests are happy; hope has became reality, and our wishes are all fulfilled." And another chimed in: "Let the groom and his young wife, as one, like the handle and the chain of the betel

stand, be free from misfortune and kept out of harm's way. Let them be granted gold in abundance, and a garden teeming with children."

While the men bandied poems about, the women distributed the nine kinds of cake sent by the *bako*, the husband's uncles and aunts, as a token of their wealth and respect: rice spiced with tamaris; cornets filled with coconut and *galamai*, a cake with rice flour and coconut milk, an *adat* symbol of the delights of marriage.

Though in the eyes of Islamic law, they were married at the religious ceremony held the previous day, Levina Rosa and Abdul Aziz could not consummate their union before the completion of the matrimonial rituals imposed by *adat*. Converts to Islam since the sixteenth century, Minangkabaus are ardent Muslims. They have nonetheless found a way to reconcile a matrilinear system derived from *adat* with Islamic principles more closely associated with a social structure of a patriarchal type. "Islam commands what has to be done, while *adat* stipulates how it should be done," Minangkabaus often say, thereby implying that the *adat* governing their every action derives from Qur'anic doctrines. *Adat* wedding rituals thus alternate with those imposed by Islam.

For instance, the premarital ceremony called *malam bainai*—an intimate, moving farewell to virginity from which the husband is excluded—is *adat*. One after the other, seven women, selected from among the bride's friends and relations, sprinkle water over the fiancée's hands and feet in an act of purification: each gesture evokes some episode from childhood and urges the bride to respect her husband-to-be and to remember her mother; finally, the women paint

The bridal procession makes its way to the bridegroom's house. She is greeted by tamaris rice thrown like confetti.

FOLLOWING PAGES
Levina Rosa awaits the arrival of her husband beside her *sumandan*.

the bride's nails with henna, an unmistakable sign that she is now betrothed. By contrast, the ceremony of *nikah*, the official sanction of the union before the *kadi*, at which the spouses' assent is read and rings exchanged, reflects the tenets of Islam.

The house had been cleared of its furniture and the floor covered with thick carpets on which had been laid tablecloths laden with food. Following tradition, the walls had been hung with cloths in three colors: red, the symbol of courage; yellow, an emblem of prosperity; and finally black, representing authority and steadfastness. At the back of the room, a *palaminan* had been set up, a kind of canopy formerly reserved for the weddings of monarchs and nobles, which today serves as an ersatz bridal alcove, itself a Minang fertility symbol. Such decorations, clearly marked by Chinese influences, are a reminder of the regular trade that used to ply between the Minangkabaus and Chinese merchants.

One legend tells of a Chinese emperor who seven times requested the hand of Bundo Kanduang, Queen of the Minangkabaus. Each time, he accompanied his suit with a present as a token of his love. His last gift was the ornament for the royal canopy, but while the precious silks were on their way to the Isle of Gold, the emperor passed away. Since that time, silk and brocade have been used to decorate the matrimonial canopy in memory of the generosity of a Chinese emperor. The decor on the *palaminan* reads like an *adat* lesson-book.

The gold-embroidered cushions placed beside the couple symbolize the mutual support they owe each other; a butterfly embroidered on a festoon reminds the bride that a virtuous housewife should be like a butterfly, a beautifully shining example to the whole community. The motif embroidered on another cushion, which shows a burgeoning tendril winding around itself, instructs fathers how to raise their children while simultaneously taking care of their sisters' offspring; the tongues of cloth resembling ties that hang down from the canopy remind the couple to pay attention to the language they use; while the silk curtains draped behind the marriage seat (the higher a couple's social class, the more curtains there are) command that the husband control his carnal desires for a few days before consummating the marriage. A traditional *adat* ceremony requires of the groom that he spend the first few nights after the wedding with his wife in the presence of a chaperon—at one time, this role was entrusted to an elderly relation who would sleep beneath the matrimonial bed to ensure the marriage was not consummated prematurely. The husband was expected to speak to his new bride all night and then leave her house at dawn to return to his mother's. The couple's life together only properly began after the *basandiang*, a sumptuous reception that concludes the wedding. As the father of a bride from Pandang explained to us, this ceremony allows Minangkabaus "to be kings, if only for a day."

Gold is to be seen everywhere: on ornaments, on clothes, and particularly on the *suntiang*, the Chinese-inspired headdress for which Sumatran brides are famous even in the West. A symbol of the burden of responsibility which weighs on women in a matrilinear society such as the Minangkabau, the *suntiang* is a diadem adorned with golden ornaments in the form of flowers, birds, and stars, arranged in a fan like a peacock's tail. Beneath her heavy headdress (it weighs more than ten pounds), a Minang bride can neither turn nor lower her head and has to remain motionless for hours at a time

The decoration and ornaments on the *palaminan* possess symbolic significance. The number of silk hangings is indicative of the spouses' social class.

beside her husband with scarcely a smile, keeping her eyes lowered like a queen and thanking all the guests awaiting their turn to pay their respects to the couple.

On the day of the *basandiang*, Levina Rosa's house was packed with people. The men and women, kept rigorously apart, were seated before the tablecloth spread with delicacies while mothers tried to control their over-exuberant offspring eager to get at the brightly colored gelatin candy shaped like teddy bears. Heralded by the banging of gongs—or *talempong*—Abdul Aziz, in a golden tunic and trousers, now appeared at the threshold. Levina Rosa's mother bowed low, took a bronze jug and sprinkled a few drops of water over his feet in welcome. Abdul Aziz inclined forward slightly too, displaying the little silver purse containing betel, without which a groom forfeits the right to enter the bride's house. Then, barefoot, Abdul Aziz crossed a white carpet—a path that symbolizes the new life and thus brings good luck—and rejoined his queen.

Various episodes from the religious ceremony called the *nikah*.

The bride's hair is dressed in a traditional style typical of the Straits of Solok.

During the *nikah*, the bride and groom exchange wedding rings and listen to the sermon by the *kadi* and speeches by the guests.

The couple and their parents on a decorated
podium during the *basandiang*, the
reception that concludes the wedding.

The bride wearing a *suntiang* weighing
more than twelve pounds.

The spouses accepting their guests'
congratulations and watching dances
performed in their honor.

GLOSSARY

INDONESIA (MINANGKABAU)

adat: rules governing Minangkabau conduct

bako: the husband's father's siblings

basandiang: marriage reception

cadiak pandai: the wise men of the village

cerano: a copper vessel containing ingredients for chewing betel

galamai: a typical traditional cake, a symbol of the joys of marriage

itiak pulang patang: "ducks returning home;" a decorative motif seen on fabrics and on houses

luah: district

malam bainai: a prenuptial ceremony of farewell to the family

nikah: religious marriage rite held at the mosque or at the bride's house

palaminan: nuptial podium or canopy

pangulu: clan chief

rumah adat or *rumah gadang:* traditional house with a roof shaped like a buffalo horn

songket: ceremonial fabric weft in gold or silver

sumandan: bridal attendants chosen from among the married women of the family

suntiang: golden diadem worn by the spouse

takuluak: brocade headdress in the shape of buffalo horns

takuluak emas: gold-painted wooden headwear

talempong: a set of bronze or copper gongs

ulama: spiritual leader

CHINA (BLACK MIAO AND SMALL FLOWERY MIAO)

laran: word designating the technique of batik

lusheng: woodwind instrument played by the Guizhou Miaos

phan: mythological bird among the Miaos

you fan: the art of seduction

Tiaohuapo: dances performed in a flowery meadow

INDIA (TAMIL)

aarti: a clockwise hand gesture intended to summon up a divinity as a witness

Agni-pradakshina: rite by which Agni, the goddess of fire, is called to witness a wedding

bindior: a spot at the middle of the forehead worn solely by married Indian women

dhoti: waistcloth worn by men

ghee: clarified butter

kanakambaram: little orange flowers

kolam: a good-luck charm drawn by women on ceremonial and festival days

kum kum: red powder used for make-up

malligai: common jasmine

mandap: place where the couple about to take their marriage vows sit before the sacred fire

mangalsutra: a thread of braided yellow silk to which is attached a gold pendant worn by married women

mullai: a variety of jasmine

Parvati: Hindu divinity, wife of Shiva

rakoli: circular jewel worn in the middle of the hair on the nape of the neck

samskara: rituals of purification that mark the various stages of Hindu life

saptapadi: the nuptial rite of the "seven paces"

sindoor: red powder streaked down the middle parting worn by married women

thalai: gold or pearl and gemstone diadem

tika: a spot in the middle of the forehead applied with *kum kum* as a sign of blessing

vagdanam: the engagement ceremony

varmala: a ritual during which the spouses exchange garlands of flowers

TIBET

borchen: large-sized silver nails

chakra: the Wheel of Life

chang: fermented barley beverage

charma: belt

dri: female of the yak

gao: gold and silver reliquary

khata: white silk scarf, worn as a good-luck charm

losar: large silver medallion

nathag tak: gifts presented by the bride's parents

nyenpo: an eminent personage of the husband's family

pöden: bejeweled Tibetan headdress

NIGER BORORO AND TUAREG

ahalu: iron-pointed utensil used by Tuareg women to dig holes for tent-poles

azalay: Tuareg ritual that marks the spouses' change of residence and the beginning of their life together

barkehi: tree of good fortune

cure salée: see *salty cure*

daddo: a kind of initiation school among the Bororos that offers teaching in relationships between the sexes

djinns: evil genies of the desert

geerewol: dance that gives its name to an assembly during which men of two clans compete in a "beauty contest"

gris-gris: talismans

ilugan: camel procession or cortege

inaden: blacksmith

karmari: a white paste, an important component in Bororo face-painting

kel-essuf: genies of the desert

koobgal: endogamous wedding arranged by the families involved

kore: Bororo word designating children betrothed at a young age

kori: dry riverbed

marabout: man of religion

wadi: dry, sandy riverbed

pura: yellow ochre

ruume: dance performed in a circle by Bororos of the same lineage that takes place during both the *worso* and the *geerewol*

salty cure: period during which Bororo herds are taken to graze in regions rich in salt (*cure salée*)

samri: man overseeing the young *sukaabe*

sukaabes: young men aged between 15 and 35 permitted to take part in the dances

sura: one of the 114 chapters of the Qur'an

surbaabe: young Bororo women

tagelmoust: Tuareg veil

taggalt: bride-price

takuba: sword

tamagsoit: red clay paste for softening the skin

Tamacheq: the language of the Tuareg

teegal: a marriage involving a couple from two different lineages, either freely entered into or the result of an elopement

tende: mortar made into a drum by being stretched with a goatskin

togu: charm among the Peulh Bororos

Wodaabe: another name for the Peulh Bororo

worso: annual gathering at which births and marriages are celebrated

yake: dance of seduction at which men of two or more bloodlines compete in a single row

MOROCCO (FASSI AND BERBER)

abroc: red silk hooded veil worn by Berber brides

ahidus: Berber dance during which men and women face each other in two rows

ahwash: Berber dance performed in a circle

ammaria: sedan-chair

asbig n iquazzain: twelve-pointed silver bracelets worn by Ait Atta women

baraka: luck, good fortune

chabba: crystal

djellaba: long hooded tunic

dawra: ritual during which the married couple is carried about on sedan-chairs

fakir: man of religion

fatiha: prayer made at the opening and closing of the Qur'an which ratifies decisions taken in the Islamic world

glissa: seat on which the bride sits during the henna ceremony

hammam: steam bath

hinna: henna

hshuma: untranslatable term that signifies both modesty and shame

hna: peace

hnana: tenderness

izar: veil worn with the caftan

jawhar: pearl-incrusted garment

khirb: heavy brocade garment in three colors (gold, white, and red or green) worn with the pearl dress

kith el-rih: "thread of the wind" frontal

lebba: large piece of jewelry comprising rows of silver-gilt drops that covers the bust

lluban: amber

maalma: form of address used by her assistants to refer to the *neggafa*

mezwarat: first wives

mida: sedan-chair employed at the *dawra*

neggafa: literally, "she who knows," responsible for organizing weddings and marriage ceremonies

neqqasha: professional specializing in applying henna

nowassi: textile bands embroidered in gold and pearls that encircles the bride's head

oud: sandalwood

saanaa: the oldest of the *neggafa*'s assistants

selta: twist of pearls adorning the hairline

serwal: cotton pantaloons secured under the knee

sharghina: plant possessing prophylactic powers

siwak: red lip stain made of the skin from the walnut root

tellunt: term applied to both the flour sieve and a goatskin drum

tkhmel: necklace made from a chain of tiny golden cylinders

wazira: a friend of the bride who serves as a witness and assistant

zgharit or *youyous:* trills performed by women that accompany all joyous celebrations

zrair: pearl-incrusted ribbons placed around a Fassi bride's face

LAPLAND

gallokak: reindeer-skin boots

joik: lyric poem sung en solo and *a capella*

lappu: the "extreme edge"

BIBLIOGRAPHY

Amrouche, Fadhma (trans. Dorothy Blair). *My Life Story: Autobiography of a Berber Woman.* New Brunswick: Rutgers University Press, 1989.

Baldizzone, Gianni, and Tiziana Baldizzone. *Tribes of India.* New Delhi: Bookwise, 2000.

— *Tibet: Journey to the Forbidden City. In the Footsteps of Alexandra David-Neel.* New York: Stewart, Tabori and Chang, 1997.

— *Tales from the River Brahmaputra: Tibet, India and Bangladesh.* Boston: Shambhala Publishing, 1998.

Beach, Hugo. *A Year in Lapland: Guest of the Reindeer Herders.* Seattle: University of Washington Press, 2000.

Beckwith, Carol. *Nomads of Niger.* New York: H.N. Abrams, 1983.

Bocquene, Henri. *Memoirs of a Mbororo.* Oxford: Berghahn, 2001.

Brick, Oussaid (trans. Ann Woollcombe). *Mountains Forgotten by God: Story of a Moroccan Berber Family.* Washington, D.C.: Three Continents Press, 1989.

Corrigan, Gina. *Miao Textiles from China.* Seattle: University of Washington Press, 2001.

Guanya, Zhu (trans. Wang Rongda). *Clothings and Ornaments of China's Miao People.* Beijing: Nationality Press, 1985.

Hart, David. *Tribe and Society in Rural Morocco.* Portland, OR: Frank Cass, 2000.

Keenan, Jeremy. *The Tuareg: People of Ahaggar.* London: Allen Lane, 1977.

Krishna, Nanditha. *Arts and Crafts of Tamilnadu.* Middletown, NJ: Grantha, 1992.

Nabokov, Isabelle. *Religion against the Self: an Ethnography of Tamil Rituals.* Oxford: Oxford University Press, 2000.

Nicolaisen, Johannes. *The Pastoral Tuareg: Ecology, Culture and Society.* New York: Thames and Hudson, 1997.

Schein, Louisa. *Minority Rules: the Miao and the Feminine in China's Cultural Politics.* Durham: Duke University Press, 2001.

Singh, Raghubir. *Tamil Nadu.* New York: Distributed Art Publishers, 1996.

Sironi Diemberger, Maria Antonia. *Tibet: The Roof of the World Bewteen Past and Present.* Boston: Shambhala Publishing, 2000.

Slavin, Kenneth. *The Tuareg.* London: Gentry Books, 1973.

Summerfield, Anne (ed.) *Walk in Splendor: Ceremonial Dress and the Minangkabau.* Los Angeles: UCLA Fowler Museum, 1999.

— *Fabled Cloths of Minangkabau.* Santa Barbara: Santa Barbara Museum of Art, 1997.

ACKNOWLEDGMENTS

We would like to offer our thanks to all the married couples and fiancés who were kind enough to allow us to attend their weddings and take photographs.

In spite of our best efforts to remain discreet, a book such as this represents something of an intrusion into one of the most special moments of a couple's life. For this reason we shall remain eternally grateful to Sarangan and Jothi, Levina Rosa and Yulfariki Abdul Aziz, Ressa and Keke, Rosa Dina and Syaharial Sakni, Rini and Jyan, Raymond and Gusria, Fatima and Brahim, Melika and Abdul, Wu Mejying and Mojian, Marit Inga and Johan Aslak, Pema and Nyma Tashi, Zhang Fa Xi, Wang Shun Qin and the Small Flowery Miaos, Fatma and Mohammed, Fedu, Jika, and all the *sukaabe*s and *surbaabe*s of the Bikorawa, Kasasawa and Djamparem lineages.

We would also like to thank their families for their welcome and for the way they took us into their homes.

We would also like to extend special thanks the following individuals:

In Indonesia: Zainal Bakar SH, the Governor of West Sumatra for all the support he offered, Dr. H. Shofwan Karim for his friendship and his inestimable help, and the Bupati of Tanah Datar Masriadi Martunus and his family for the generous and warm hospitality they offered us at Batusangkar and Lintau. Al Busyra Basnur at the Indonesian Embassy in Rome, Yusman Kasim, Dr. Hasrin Mansyur and the Tourist Office of West Sumatra, Syofyani Yusaf and her dance troop, Putri Bulqish Shofwan, our friend Maria Felisia Tjoa, all the couples' families, Datuk Gindo Rustam Sharif and family, Ir. Mudrika and family, Ir. Man Nas K Sulaiman S.sos and family, the Syahmenan family, HJ. Masnur Lukman, Antonia Soriente, Yal Darwis SH, and Arifin.

In India: our friends Malathi and Rama Ramaswami and the Indebo Agency in New Delhi, Suniti Narayan, Smt. Gayathri Sankar and Lt. Col. J.Sankar, Smt. Rajam Narayanamurthy and Sri L. R. Narayanamurthy, Maj. Gen. A. Balasubhramanian.

In Niger: Rissa Ag Boulla, Minister of Tourism, our friend Ghalidou Mahoumoudane and his agency Air Voyage of Agadez for his prompt assistance, the Director General of the Ministery of Tourism at Niamey, Alberto Nicheli and Transafrica, Moussa Aouarakum, and Hasan, our very good Wodaabe friend.

In Morocco: Mohamed Melehi, Henia Chikhaoui Trachène, Conservator at the Batha Museum at Fez, for time and assistance so readily offered, the Director of the Tourist Information Office at Fez, Metiri Mohamed, Samia Menjili, the *neggafa* Hadja el Batoul and her assistants in Fez, Atrash Naima at Asilah, Mehdi El Abbadi and La Maison Bleue, Fez, Ikrame Alami, Lebbar Abdelmalek, Idir Ougunir, Lahcen M'Hamdi, and Bahssine Ali.

In China: Sun Hong at the Guyang CITS, Zhang Tsai Xiu, Zhu Yueng Zhen, Wang Jiaying, Zhang Fu Fin, and Mojian and Wu Meijing's families.

In Norway: Inger Marie Olino Gaino, Kirsten Berit, Ragnhild Nystad, Member of the Sami Parliament, Maria Laakfo of the Tourist Information Office of Enontekio, May Kirsti Turi and the Karasjok Oppelvelser.

In Tibet: all our friends among the Kham, most especially Nyima Tsering and Rinchin Drolma.

Thanks too to Julie Rouart and Axel Buret for all their hard work and enthusiasm during the making of this book, and last, but not least, thanks to our friend Carla Milone Parato for logistical support in organizing our travels.

MfiPl- 8/25

3 1221 07192 9975